God's Handbook

Learn To Use The Bible To Answer All Of Life's Most Difficult Questions!

K. W. Oliver

508

FIVE O' EIGHT
PUBLISHING

ISBN-13:978-0692395059
ISBN-10:0692395059
Second Edition, First Printing, 2025

DEDICATION

As in all that I do, **I dedicate this book to God.**
But I would like to thank my family for their
unwavering support. My wife, Karla, you are how I
know God loves me. Mom and Dad, thank you for
instilling the word of God in my life
and never giving up on me.
I couldn't ask for better brothers than Steven,
Thomas, and Calvin. Your friendship, loyalty, and
love. Accepted me when no one would.
Defended me when no one could,
and loved me when no one should.
Thank You!

CONTENTS

PROLOGUE

When I first released this book in 2015, my heart was simple: to help believers and seekers alike discover that God's Word already holds the answers to life's most difficult questions. I wanted to point people past my words and toward the true Author — God Himself.

Now, ten years later, I've seen even more clearly how desperately we need God's wisdom today. The world has changed. Life feels louder, faster, and more divided than ever before. People are carrying more fear, anxiety, and uncertainty than at any time I can remember. But here's the good news: God has not changed. His Word is still as true, powerful, and relevant as it was when He first gave it.

That's why this 2025 updated edition exists. Some content has been reorganized. Some sections have been rewritten. And new insights have been added to address challenges many of us are facing today. But one thing hasn't changed — my prayer for you.

My Prayer for You

I'm praying that this book becomes more than just words on a page for you.
I pray that you don't lean on your own understanding of the world or on the shifting voices of culture, but instead learn to trust God's Word as your ultimate guide.

I'm praying for a revival in your spiritual life — that

God would breathe fresh strength into your faith, open your eyes to His promises, and renew your hope in Him.

I don't know your story. I don't know what brought you to this book today. But I do know this: God knows you. He sees every struggle, every victory, every unanswered question, and every silent prayer. And if you're holding this book right now, I believe it's no accident.

Why I Wrote This Book

This book was born out of my own frustration. For years, I had questions about my walk with Christ — deep, personal questions — but I couldn't seem to find clear, practical answers. I had been a Christian most of my life, yet I constantly felt like I was missing something.

I went to pastors. I joined Bible studies. I listened to sermons. And though people genuinely tried to help, the answers often felt vague, incomplete, or ended with: "Just pray about it."

Prayer is powerful — but I needed direction.

Eventually, God opened my eyes: I had been putting my hope in people instead of Him. I was looking for answers in places where they didn't exist. That realization changed everything.

I began reading the Bible differently — not just for inspiration, but with a deep belief that God's Word already contained the answers I was seeking. And I discovered something life-changing:

When you stop relying on people to do what only God can do,
You finally make space to hear His voice.

The Bible — God's Living Instruction Manual

When I was a child, my mother would always say:

"All you need to know is in the Bible."

Back then, I didn't fully understand it. But now, I can tell you from experience — she was right.

People often say, "Life doesn't come with an instruction manual." But that's simply not true. God has already given us one.

Inside Scripture, we find wisdom for every part of life:

How to build a godly marriage.

How to overcome fear, anxiety, and depression.

How to handle grief, regret, and loss.

How to make decisions with clarity and peace.

How to live with purpose, hope, and joy.

Every answer we truly need is there — we just need

to know where to look.

What to Expect From This Updated Edition

This isn't just a re-release. It's a renewal.
In this 2025 edition, I've:

Reorganized the chapters for better flow and clarity.

Expanded sections to address modern struggles we
face in today's world.

Added new insights, prayers, and tools to help you
apply God's Word more effectively.

But the heart of the book hasn't changed: to point
you to God's Word — not my opinions, not the
shifting wisdom of culture, but the unchanging truth
of Scripture.

No matter what you're walking through, I believe
God can use this book to draw you closer to Him. My
prayer is that, by the time you reach the last page,
you'll have more than answers — you'll have a deeper
relationship with the One who wrote them

CHAPTER 1
HOW TO READ THE BIBLE

For many people, the **Bible** can feel intimidating. It's big, ancient, sometimes hard to understand, and — let's be honest — there are moments when it might even feel **boring**. You're not alone if you've felt this way.

Some people assume that because the Bible was written thousands of years ago, it must be outdated or irrelevant. But that couldn't be further from the truth. **The Bible is alive**. It speaks today as powerfully as it did when it was first written. God didn't give us an ancient manual that stopped working when technology advanced. He gave us **timeless wisdom** for every generation — including this one.

You may drive a car, send text messages, and fly on airplanes, but God's Word is **still relevant** to your life today. As Psalm 139:16 says:

"Your eyes saw my unformed body; all the days ordained for me were written in your book before one of them came to be."

Before you were born, God already knew you. Jesus even says in Matthew 10:30:

"Even the very hairs of your head are all numbered."

That means He knows every detail of your life. If the Creator of the universe knows you this intimately, do you really think He would leave you with an **outdated** guide for how to live? Absolutely not.

The Bible is **eternal truth**. It was written for you, right now, in the middle of **this** moment in history. And when you approach it with that understanding, it will change everything.

Step One: Understand What the Bible Really Is

One of the biggest mistakes new readers make is treating the Bible like any other book — opening to page one, starting in Genesis, and expecting to read straight through to Revelation.

But the Bible **isn't one single book**. It's a **collection of 66 books** written by more than 40 different people over thousands of years — yet it tells one **consistent story**: God's plan to redeem humanity.

Think of the Bible as a **miniature library**. Inside, you'll find:

- **History** — the story of God's people and His faithfulness
- **Poetry & Wisdom** — Psalms, Proverbs, and writings full of encouragement and guidance
- **Prophecy** — messages pointing to Jesus and God's promises
- **Biographies** — eyewitness accounts of Jesus' life and ministry
- **Letters** — instructions and encouragement for followers of Christ

And here's what makes this library unique: **every word is God-breathed**.

"All Scripture is given by inspiration of God, and is profitable for doctrine, for reproof, for correction, and for instruction in righteousness, that the man of God may be complete, thoroughly equipped for every good work."
(2 Timothy 3:16-17)

The Bible isn't just **about** God's words — it **is** God's Word. It's His primary way of speaking to you today

.

Step Two: Choose the Right Translation

Since the Bible is the most widely published book in history, there are dozens of translations available. Some are designed to be very literal, while others focus on readability and flow.

For beginners, I recommend starting with:

- **ESV (English Standard Version)** — accurate, clear, and balanced.
- **NLT (New Living Translation)** — easy to understand and very approachable.
- **CSB (Christian Standard Bible)** — highly readable and faithful to the original text.

You may also enjoy paraphrased versions like **The Message (MSG)**, which summarize ideas more conversationally, but I wouldn't rely on those alone for deep study.

The most important thing is this: **find a translation you'll actually read**. If you're uncomfortable with the wording or style, you'll avoid opening it. Go to a bookstore, browse a few versions, and find one that speaks to you clearly.

Step Three: Don't Start at the Beginning

This one surprises people, but if you're new to reading the Bible, starting at **Genesis 1:1** can feel overwhelming. The Bible is a library, so we don't have to start at "page one."

I recommend beginning with the **New Testament**, especially one of the four Gospels — Matthew, Mark, Luke, or John. These books give you a direct view of Jesus' life, teachings, miracles, death, and resurrection — the foundation of everything we believe.

Step Four: A Two-Week Bible Reading Plan

Here's a simple two-week plan to introduce you to the Bible's core message. Just one chapter per day — five to ten minutes each:

Day 1 – Luke 1: Preparing for Jesus' arrival
Day 2 – Luke 2: The story of Jesus' birth
Day 3 – Mark 1: The beginning of Jesus' ministry
Day 4 – Mark 9: A day in the life of Jesus
Day 5 – Matthew 5: The Sermon on the Mount
Day 6 – Matthew 6: The Sermon on the Mount continued
Day 7 – Luke 15: Parables of Jesus
Day 8 – John 3: A conversation with Jesus
Day 9 – John 14: Jesus' final instructions
Day 10 – John 17: Jesus' prayer for His disciples
Day 11 – Matthew 26: Betrayal and arrest
Day 12 – Matthew 27: The crucifixion
Day 13 – John 20: The resurrection
Day 14 – Luke 24: Jesus appears after His resurrection

(Adapted from the New Student Bible, 1992 NIV edition.)

Step Five: Let the Bible Speak to You

Finally, remember this: the Bible isn't just meant to be read — it's meant to be **lived**.

When you open Scripture, **invite God into the process**. Pray before you begin:

"Lord, open my eyes. Show me what You want me to see. Help me understand and apply Your Word."

Approach the Bible not as an academic assignment, but as a personal conversation with the Creator of the universe. The more you read, the more you'll realize something incredible: **God is speaking directly to you.**

CHAPTER 2
HOW TO WALK WITH CHRIST

Developing your walk with Christ is one of the most important things you can do. It should go without saying that learning *how* to walk with Christ is just as important. When I say "walking with Christ," I'm talking about your relationship with Jesus.

Does it seem odd that we would have a personal relationship with Christ? I hope not. Rekindling our relationship with Christ reconnects us with God. Originally, in the Garden of Eden, God had a deep, personal relationship with Adam and Eve. That wasn't by mistake either—God designed us to communicate with Him regularly.

Unfortunately, sin got in the way (as it usually does). After Adam and Eve sinned, they hid from God. They didn't want to talk to Him or even see Him. They were ashamed of what they did. Not only were they ashamed, but they were also frightened of how God would respond to their actions.

In my opinion, sin is the most corruptive force there is. It single-handedly broke our relationship with God. That relationship can be restored, but it will take some work. Building a relationship with Christ, in turn, strengthens our relationship with God—they are, after all, one and the same: Father, Son, and Holy Spirit.

John 14:6 – *"Jesus said to him, 'I am the way, and the truth, and the life. No one comes to the Father except through Me.'"*

Why Should We Have a Relationship with Christ?

Aside from the obvious benefits of having God as your friend, we should have a relationship with Christ because we love Him—and we love Him because He first loved us.

1 John 4:19 – *"We love because He first loved us."*

When we love someone, we naturally want to be around that person. It's enjoyable to be near those we love. Our walk with Christ will grow naturally as our love for Him grows. However, just as in every relationship, the honeymoon only lasts so long. Eventually, we need to begin working on the relationship. Friendships take effort—or eventually, you start to drift apart.

Have you ever had a friend you simply lost contact with? It wasn't anything either of you did on purpose; it just kind of happened. The relationship was no longer a priority. That's what we need to avoid with Christ.

How to Have a Relationship with Christ

Your relationship with Christ began the moment you were saved. Whether you've taken advantage of that relationship or not is another matter. If you haven't been intentionally walking with Christ, start today. Make the choice to pick up your cross and follow Him.

Your friendship with Christ is no different than any other relationship you have in life—it takes work. If you don't work at your relationships, eventually they will fall apart. That means seeking out Christ. Just as you would call a friend to say hello, we need to go to God in prayer and worship.

The best time to do that is when you first wake up. I know we all live busy lives, and waking up fifteen minutes early doesn't sound appealing. But the Bible says:

1 Peter 5:8 – *"The devil prowls around like a roaring lion, seeking someone to devour."*

The adversary is waiting at the foot of your bed every morning. He would love nothing more than to have you focus on yourself instead of Christ. You have to plan to go to God every day. That includes prayer, worship, and spending time in His Word.

Just wake up fifteen minutes early, open your Bible, and read one or two chapters. That simple act goes a long way toward starting your day right. Then continue your daily routine with the mindset of focusing on Christ while you're doing it.

When you get in the shower, turn on some worship music and praise Him. As you're getting dressed, think about the Scriptures you just read. While you're eating breakfast, talk to Him about the things that trouble you. On the way to work, turn the praise music on again. Spending your morning with God is an awesome way to start the day—and it strengthens your relationship with Him.

Get Involved with the Body of Christ

The next part of walking with Christ is getting involved with the body of Christ—the church. If you're not part of a good, Bible-believing church, you need to be.

Finding the right church is like finding a good pair of jeans: you may have to try a few on. If you've lived in your community for any length of time, you've likely seen several churches around. Stop in and see what the congregation is like. Are they friendly? Did someone greet you at the door? Are people smiling?

Talk with the pastor. See if they have any literature about the church, perhaps a *statement of faith* that lays out what they believe. Don't be shy about asking questions. It's important that the church aligns as closely as possible with the Word of God—allow yourself to be led by the Holy Spirit.

Once you're attending a good, Bible-believing church regularly, it's time to get involved. Begin looking for a place to serve. Pray about it, and ask the leadership in your church what openings they have.

Why is it important to serve in the church? In my own life, my relationship with Christ really began to grow when I started serving Him. What better place to begin serving God than in His house?

Serving not only lets you see how others serve Christ but also how they walk with Him. This helps us identify areas in our own walk that need improvement. That reflection is part of the overall design of the body of Christ.

Hebrews 10:25 – *"Not neglecting to meet together, as is the habit of some, but encouraging one another—and all the more as you see the Day drawing near."*

Make Time for Christ

Remember, this is about *your* walk with Christ—not Christ's walk with you. Jesus is the perfect friend; He's always by our side. He loves you and wants to communicate with you through His Holy Spirit. All you have to do is make time for Him.

The more time you spend with Christ, the closer your walk will be. If you don't make time for this relationship, nothing else in this book will help you. Everything hangs on your relationship with God.

Make it a priority. Set time aside in the morning and in the evening. Start your day in prayer and worship, continue it relying on God's strength, and end it in thankfulness.

CHAPTER 3
HOW TO LEAD SOMEONE TO CHRIST

Leading someone to Christ is a lot like leading a horse to water—you can lead them to water, but you can't make them drink. You can evangelize your family and friends until you're blue in the face, but if they don't want to accept the living water that is Jesus Christ, you can't make them.

Each one of us is called to salvation.

John 6:44 – *"No one can come to Me unless the Father who sent Me draws him. And I will raise him up on the last day."*

The Father calls each one of us individually, and individually it's up to us to answer that call. The word "draw" in the verse above is interesting. The Greek word translated *draw* is *helkuo*, which means "to drag" (literally or figuratively).

Helkuo is used in **John 21:6** to refer to a heavy net full of fish being dragged to the shore. In **John 18:10**, Peter draws his sword, and in **Acts 16:19**, *helkuo* describes Paul and Silas being dragged into the marketplace before the rulers.

I think this describes the conversion process rather nicely. For myself, I was drawn figuratively to Christ as a moth to a flame—gently, warmly, almost hypnotically. It began as a strong curiosity, almost an infatuation. However, some resist God's call and must be dragged like a heavy net of fish into the boat, or like Paul and Silas into the marketplace.

Our loving God does this because it's impossible for us to do it ourselves. Our sinful nature is so strong that we are not able to overcome it to find God—and without His grace, we wouldn't even have the desire to do so.

Why God Designed It This Way

Ephesians 2:8-10 – *"For by grace you have been saved through faith. And this is not your own doing; it is the gift of God, not a result of works, so that no one may boast. For we are His workmanship, created in Christ Jesus for good works, which God prepared beforehand, that we should walk in them."*

Salvation is a gift. Our pride is so perverted and strong that we want to claim salvation as our own doing: *"I made the decision to come to Christ."* In truth, we play no part in our own salvation; however, we can play a part in someone else's.

Be Christlike

One of the best ways we can lead someone to Christ is by being Christlike. We should live our lives as examples to the rest of the world. There's something powerful about being in close proximity to a mature Christian who's simply living their faith—it speaks to people, even if they can't quite explain why.

Matthew 5:16 – *"In the same way, let your light shine before others, so that they may see your good works and give glory to your Father who is in heaven."*

Living as an example gives you opportunities to talk about Christ. One of the most effective ways to do that is by sharing your testimony—how you came to know Christ, what He's done for you, and how He's changed your life.

We should all be ready to give our testimony at any time. You never know who God may want you to share it with—a friend, a coworker, or even a stranger in line. Stay open to the Holy Spirit, and when the time comes, He'll give you the words to say.

Pray for the Resistant

When it comes to close friends or family who seem resistant to God's call, prayer is essential. We should pray that God would call them into His Kingdom and that they would be open and receptive to His voice.

Prayer should never be underestimated—it's a powerful gift that allows us to communicate directly with our Lord. Take advantage of what God has given you. Make your petitions known to Him, and He will be faithful in answering them.

Philippians 4:6 – *"Do not be anxious about anything, but in everything by prayer and supplication with thanksgiving let your requests be made known to God."*

Don't be overbearing. Constantly pounding on their door with warnings of hellfire won't help. As Christ's followers, we should leave a *sweet taste* in people's mouths. Bring up Christ naturally in conversation— it's more organic and far less forced. Remember, we're trying to *draw* people, not push them away.

How to Get Saved

Some years ago, I wrote on the topic of salvation in a short piece titled **"How to Get Saved."** I've included it here in full. I pray it will be useful to you.

Understanding Salvation

Salvation isn't complicated. There are no trials to face or ancient ceremonies to perform. For the most part, salvation happens privately—it takes less than sixty seconds, and it's between you and God alone.

It can help to have a Christian friend lead you in prayer, but ultimately, salvation is a personal moment of surrender.

What Is Salvation?

Salvation is Jesus stepping in and accepting your punishment.

Punishment? you might say. *I'm a good person. I try to live right. I donate to charity and help my family and friends. Why would I deserve punishment?*

It's not just you—we all do. Every one of us deserves punishment for the sins we've committed, no matter how good we are or how hard we try.

Leviticus 19:11 – *"Do not steal. Do not lie. Do not deceive one another."*

We all fall short of the glory of God. Have you ever told a lie, even a "white" one? Taken something small from work? That's sin.

You might say, *So you're telling me because I stole a pencil, I have to spend eternity in hell?* Of course not—but that's not the only thing you've done. It's a lifetime accumulation of sin that must be answered for.

Not all sins are the same in severity, but the punishment for sin is the same.

Romans 6:23 – *"For the wages of sin is death, but the gift of God is eternal life in Christ Jesus our Lord."*

It doesn't say *the wages of big sin*—it says *the wages of sin.* That means any sin leads to death, not physical death, but spiritual separation from God. The place of eternal separation is called hell.

The bright side of Romans 6:23 is this: *"The gift of God is eternal life in Christ Jesus our Lord."* God doesn't want anyone to end up in hell. Because He is just, sin must still be paid for. That's where Jesus comes in.

John 3:16-18 – *"For God so loved the world that He gave His one and only Son, that whoever believes in Him shall not perish but have eternal life. For God did not send His Son into the world to condemn the world, but to save the world through Him. Whoever believes in Him is not condemned, but whoever does not believe stands condemned already because they have not believed in the name of God's one and only Son."*

God sent His only Son so that you and I could be saved. Don't rush past that—let it sink in. God loves you so much that He sent His Son to die on the cross for you.

Jesus was beaten, tortured, and convicted of crimes He didn't commit. He was utterly blameless. Like us, He was human, but unlike us, He never sinned. As He hung on the cross, He bore the full weight of the world's sins. God placed the punishment meant for you upon Him.

Matthew 27:46 – *"About three in the afternoon Jesus cried out in a loud voice, 'Eli, Eli, lema sabachthani?' (which means 'My God, My God, why have You forsaken Me?')"*

That's the punishment for sin—separation from God. What a painful sacrifice.

The Cost of Separation

Some might ask, *What's so bad about being separated from God?*

Every one of us is born with blessings we take for granted—the ability to feel joy, to enjoy life, to give and receive love. Imagine losing all of that.

James 1:17 – *"Every good and perfect gift is from above, coming down from the Father of the heavenly lights, who does not change like shifting shadows."*

Eternal separation from God means losing every good thing—and gaining pain, regret, and awareness of what was lost. Jesus illustrated this vividly:

Luke 16:19-31 – *The Rich Man and Lazarus.* (Full passage quoted in this section of your manuscript, retained for context.)

Accepting the Truth

Some people say there are "steps" to salvation. There's really only one, and it's found in **John 3:16**:

"For God so loved the world that He gave His one and only Son, that whoever believes in Him shall not perish but have eternal life."

That's it. It's that simple. All you have to do is believe that Jesus is who He says He is, that He came to save you from your sins by dying on the cross.

If you truly believe that, your life will change. You'll want to follow His teachings and repent of sin—but you can't do that on your own. You need God's help. That's where prayer comes in.

The Sinner's Prayer

This is an example prayer. You don't have to use these exact words, but you must believe them in your heart.

If you struggle to believe, start here:

"God, You know me. You know what's in my heart. I long to know the truth, but I'm having trouble discerning truth from falsehood. Please give me wisdom and guidance. Show me the one and only way to You. Speak to my heart so that when I hear the truth, I'll recognize it. Thank You. Amen."

If you prayed that prayer, trust that God will help you find Him. Now, if you're ready to accept salvation, pray this next prayer:

"Father, I thank You for sending Your one and only Son to die on the cross so that I may have eternal life. I repent of my sins and ask that You forgive me—not because I deserve it, but because I trust what Your Word says: that whoever believes Your Son died for our sins shall have eternal life. Please come into my heart and make me new. Thank You, Father. In Jesus' name, Amen."

After Someone Comes to Christ

When a person comes to know Christ, our job isn't finished—it's just begun. We are responsible for helping disciple the new believer.

We must do our best to make sure they aren't led astray by false teaching or the enemy's influence. Guard them in prayer. Lead them to a good, Bible-believing church. Provide encouragement and support. Be available to answer questions about Jesus and the Bible. It's okay if you don't know the answer—just say, *"That's a great question. Let's find out together."* Pray about it and search Scripture together.

Resources like this book are great tools to give new believers, along with a copy of the Bible. Remember that God is using you in this person's life, so set a good example of what a Christian should look like. Stay away from sin—and even the appearance of sin. Be cautious in conversations with the opposite gender; the adversary loves to tempt and destroy godly relationships.

Be bold, be loving, and in all things, remain open to the guidance of the Holy Spirit.

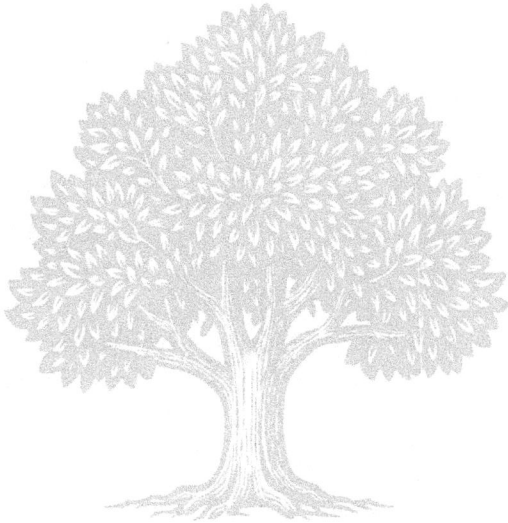

CHAPTER 4
HOW TO FIND GOD'S WILL
FOR YOUR LIFE

Most people who ask, "How do I find God's will for my life?" are looking for guidance in specific decisions. *Is it God's will that I marry this person? Should I take this job offer? Lord, should I buy the house on Apple Ridge Road or the one on Kentucky Avenue?* Let's see what the Bible says.

Understanding What God's Will Truly Is

Scripture depicts God's will in two ways. The first is **His sovereign will**.

Ephesians 1:11 – *"In Him we were also chosen, having been predestined according to the plan of Him who works out everything in conformity with the purpose of His will."*

God's sovereign will is His overarching plan for the universe and humanity. It encompasses creation itself; the birth, death, and resurrection of Jesus Christ; the promises He has made—such as salvation for you and me—judgment of the wicked, and the final punishment of Satan and his followers. In my view, His sovereign will is mostly hidden from us, though He gives us glimpses through Scripture and prophecy.

God's sovereign will cannot be changed. That's a good thing, because we don't need to worry about it—it's above our pay grade, so to speak. No matter what we do, we won't change God's mind about His sovereign will. Most of it is hidden from us anyway. Think of it like this:

A father tells his young son, "You have a soccer game this Saturday." All the son knows is that a game is coming; he doesn't concern himself with anything else. The father, however, must buy cleats, socks, and shin guards; make sure the fees are paid; ensure his son practices; and put gas in the car to get him to the game. Because it's the father's will that the son play soccer, it's the father's responsibility to provide everything needed to fulfill that will.

In the same way, because our heavenly Father has a sovereign will, He sets everything in place. What God does is infinitely more complex than buying equipment, of course—but we should be like the son and rest in the Father's care.

The second is **His moral will**—the instructions He's given us in the Bible. Unlike His sovereign will, His moral will can be disobeyed. We can choose to follow Jesus and His teachings or turn from Him and wallow in sin.

That's it? But I still don't know whether to marry this person or which house to buy—and what about that job offer?

Don't Hop the Fence

God's Word acts like a fence around a yard. It gives us clear boundaries; inside the fence, we're free to walk and enjoy what He's given. When facing a decision, apply God's Word to it.

Should I marry this person? Scripture says not to be unequally yoked. Is your partner a believer or still in sin? If the answer to the first is *yes*, you're free to marry. If *no*, you've reached the fence. You could hop it—but you'd be outside God's moral will.

What about the job offer? Does it require you to act against God's Word—shading the truth to make a sale, "padding the numbers," or compromising integrity? Then you have your answer.

Sometimes, God gives us multiple options that are equally acceptable. **Where should I live?** Wherever you like—as long as you stay inside the fence. Can you afford the property? Then go for it. Apply Scripture to the decision; that's what Romans 12:2 is about.

Romans 12:2 – *"Do not conform to the pattern of this world, but be transformed by the renewing of your mind. Then you will be able to test and approve what God's will is—His good, pleasing and perfect will."*

Is it so hard to believe it's that simple? Many of us struggle, trying to make God reveal His will for every moment. He already has.

Psalm 119:105 (NIV) – *"Your word is a lamp for my feet, a light on my path."*

God's Word illuminates the path you're on so you can see and choose wisely. If you've been praying for wisdom and clarity and haven't sensed a specific leading, pick up your Bible. God wants His Word hidden in your heart so you don't have to stop every fifteen minutes to discern His will—you'll already know it. And if it's His **sovereign** will that you be somewhere or do something, you won't be able to resist it. The pull will be so strong that you'll have no doubt. Enjoy the freedom He's given—just remember to stay inside the yard.

1 Peter 5:8 – *"Be alert and of sober mind. Your enemy the devil prowls around like a roaring lion looking for someone to devour."*

CHAPTER 5
HOW TO PUT ON
THE FULL ARMOR OF GOD

Some passages of Scripture are preached more often than others. One of those is the **armor of God** in Ephesians 6. It's a powerful text because it explains how to withstand attacks from the enemy. Unfortunately, many sermons stop at *what* the armor is and *why* it matters—but not *how* to use it. Let's walk through both.

What Is the Armor of God—and Why Do We Need It?

Ephesians 6:13–17 – *"Therefore put on the full armor of God, so that when the day of evil comes, you may be able to stand your ground, and after you have done everything, to stand. Stand firm then, with the belt of truth buckled around your waist, with the breastplate of righteousness in place, and with your feet fitted with the readiness that comes from the gospel of peace. In addition to all this, take up the shield of faith, with which you can extinguish all the flaming arrows of the evil one. Take the helmet of salvation and the sword of the Spirit, which is the word of God."*

Paul isn't talking about physical armor you can buy at a Christian bookstore. He's describing a **spiritual** suit of armor—six principles: **Truth, Righteousness, Peace, Faith, Salvation,** and **the Word of God**. He's equipping us for a real battlefield:

Ephesians 6:12 – *"For our struggle is not against flesh and blood, but against the rulers, against the authorities, against the powers of this dark world and against the spiritual forces of evil in the heavenly realms."*

So we are not fighting physical beings in a physical realm, but evil spiritual beings in a spiritual realm. That can sound unusual—even a little sci-fi—but it is true and 100% real. This is a perfect moment to lift the **shield of faith.**

Romans 10:17 – *"Consequently, faith comes from hearing the message, and the message is heard through the word about Christ."*

If you struggle with this, dig into the Word and pray for wisdom and guidance. The Lord will show you what's truly happening. We now know **what** the armor is (six principles) and **why** we need it (a spiritual battle). Here's **how** to put it on.

Gearing Up

Applying these six principles is like applying any other part of Scripture—it's simple in idea, harder in practice. Let's take them one by one.

I. The Belt of Truth

Like any belt, truth holds everything together. Here Paul points to **God's eternal truth**. The enemy's first weapon is always **lies**: *You're not really saved… God doesn't love you… You have no authority over me.* Our best defense is the truth set deep in our hearts— **Scripture**. If anything contradicts God's Word, it's a lie.

John 8:44 – *"…He was a murderer from the beginning, not holding to the truth, for there is no truth in him. When he lies, he speaks his native language, for he is a liar and the father of lies."*

II. The Breastplate of Righteousness

Accusations—whether true memories of our past or outright lies—aim for the heart. **Righteousness** guards it like a breastplate. This is not our personal righteousness or the works of men; apart from Christ we have none.

Job 25:4 – *"How then can a mortal be righteous before God? How can one born of woman be pure?"*

It is **Jesus' righteousness** that covers and protects us. In salvation, He clothes us in His righteousness and makes us stand secure.

III. The Sandals of the Gospel of Peace

"...with your feet fitted with the readiness that comes from the gospel of peace." (Eph. 6:15)

God's Word *readies* us for the battles every Christian must face, and there is **peace** in being prepared. If you read the Bible, you already know the outcome— **Christ wins**—and that assurance steadies your steps.

IV. The Shield of Faith

Satan loves to plant **doubt**. Any lingering doubt becomes a chink in the armor that he will pry open. The stronger your faith, the stronger your defense. Stand **behind** your faith—declare the truth you've heard and believed—until the flaming arrows fizzle out on the shield.

V. The Helmet of Salvation

A helmet is non-negotiable in battle. So is **salvation** if we want victory. As a helmet guards the head, salvation guards the **mind**. How we think—anchored in our identity in Christ—is crucial for resisting the enemy's schemes.

VI. The Sword of the Spirit (The Word of God)

Up to now, every piece has been **defensive**. God doesn't want us only to endure; He wants us to **overcome**. Our single **offensive** weapon is the **Word of God**—wielded as the **Sword of the Spirit**.

How can the Word be both defense and offense? It depends on *how you use it*. Jesus gives the perfect model:

Matthew 4:1–11 – Jesus is tempted in the wilderness.
• The tempter says, *"Tell these stones to become bread."* Jesus trusts the Father (faith) and answers with Scripture: *"It is written: 'Man shall not live on bread alone, but on every word that comes from the mouth of God.'"*
• The devil quotes Scripture out of context, urging Jesus to jump.
Jesus answers rightly: *"It is also written: 'Do not put the Lord your God to the test.'"*
• The devil offers the kingdoms of the world for worship.
Jesus, confident in His righteousness and authority, commands: *"Away from me, Satan! For it is written: 'Worship the Lord your God, and serve Him only.'"*

Result: *"Then the devil left Him, and angels came and attended Him."*

Jesus **parries** lies with truth and **strikes** with rightly-used Scripture. Through His righteousness and in His name, we carry that same delegated authority to resist the devil.

Don't Forget Prayer

Immediately after listing the armor, Paul adds:

Ephesians 6:18 – *"And pray in the Spirit on all occasions with all kinds of prayers and requests."*

Prayer isn't labeled as a piece of armor, but it **empowers** all the others and keeps our hearts aligned with God. Pray constantly; stay alert.

Putting It All Together (Daily Practice)

Truth: Start your day in Scripture; memorize a verse you can speak back to lies.

Righteousness: Confess sin quickly; rest in Christ's righteousness, not your performance.

Peace: Let the gospel steady your steps; rehearse the Good News.

Faith: Declare what God has said, especially when feelings lag.

Salvation: Preach your identity to yourself—*I am in Christ, forgiven, adopted, secure.*

Word of God: Answer temptation with specific Scripture—out loud if you can.

Prayer: Pray in the Spirit "on all occasions."

Stand your ground. You are fully equipped in Christ—and in His strength, you will stand.

CHAPTER 6
HOW TO PRAY

One of the most spectacular benefits of being a Christian is **prayer**. Prayer gives us a direct line to God whenever we want—no waiting in line or being put on hold. We're never asked to leave a message or call back at a more convenient time. God is never too busy for His children; in fact, He anticipates hearing from us. He loves to hear from us. As Christians, we should love to talk to our Father. Sadly, there's often confusion about how to pray properly.

As I hope you know, confusion doesn't come from God. Jesus lays out in Matthew exactly how we're supposed to pray.

Matthew 6:5–13

"And when you pray, do not be like the hypocrites, for they love to pray standing in the synagogues and on the street corners to be seen by others. Truly I tell you, they have received their reward in full."

Be Real: What Jesus is telling us is **don't pray to be heard by people**. Some love to be the center of attention—offering flashy prayers to show how "holy" they are. Jesus says people like that have already received their reward in full.

"But when you pray, go into your room, close the door and pray to your Father, who is unseen. Then your Father, who sees what is done in secret, will reward you."

Jesus tells us to go someplace private. Privacy allows you to pray aloud without fear of being overheard and helps you be more open and honest with your Father. Most of all, He says He will reward what is done in secret.

"And when you pray, do not keep on babbling like pagans, for they think they will be heard because of their many words. Do not be like them, for your Father knows what you need before you ask Him."

Be Simple: Jesus refers to pagans who repeat the same words as if many words make prayer effective. Unfortunately, some Christian traditions seem to miss this, prescribing repetitive prayers— *"Say ten Our Fathers and six Hail Marys and your sin will be forgiven."* Not only is it sad that people believe this; it's unbiblical. When you go to God in prayer, **say what you need to say—once is enough**. He already knows your needs.

"This, then, is how you should pray: 'Our Father in heaven, hallowed be Your name...'"

Be Worshipful: Jesus starts with, *"Our Father in heaven, hallowed be Your name."* He is saying, "Holy is Your name." We should begin prayer from a **posture of worship**. That doesn't necessarily mean singing— though that's not a bad idea. We worship by **expressing God's holiness and righteousness**, just as Jesus does here.

"Your kingdom come, Your will be done, on earth as it is in heaven."

Be Submissive: Scripture tells us to come **boldly** before the throne, but bold does not mean prideful. We don't give God orders— *"You're going to do this for me because I want it now!"* Jesus is submissive: *Father, let Your will be done on earth by us as quickly and perfectly as it is in heaven by Your angels.* Another way to say it: **Father, let all that I do be Your will.**

"Give us today our daily bread."

Be Practical: Jesus asks that His daily needs be met. This is where we humbly ask for what we **need**—work, healing, clothing, food, finances. We may even ask for things we **want**, remembering that our requests should be **within His will**. (So if you're at a casino praying, *"Lord, let me win big,"* you know why God didn't honor that prayer.)

"And forgive us our debts, as we also have forgiven our debtors."

Be Repentant: Jesus asks to be forgiven **as** He forgives others. We shouldn't expect God's forgiveness if we've refused to forgive those who offended us. Take time in prayer to **actively forgive** the people who have hurt you.

"And lead us not into temptation, but deliver us from the evil one."

Be Expectant: Begin to end your prayer **thankfully,** trusting that what you asked—because it aligns with God's will—will be granted according to His wisdom and timing. Many translations add a doxology:

"For Yours is the kingdom and the power and the glory forever. Amen."

It's good to **end by glorifying God**, lifting His name above all others.

CHAPTER 7
HOW TO DEAL WITH STRESS

Stress—just the thought of tackling the topic can cause some. In all seriousness, untold numbers of books have been written about stress, and a good portion of them aren't very helpful.

The physical and mental effects of stress on the human body are staggering. Below are just a few.

When We Are Stressed

- Blood pressure rises

- Breathing becomes more rapid
- Digestive system slows
- Heart rate increases
- Immune response decreases
- Muscles tense
- Sleep is disrupted (heightened alertness)

Effects on Your Body

- Excessive sweating
- Back pain
- Chest pain
- Childhood obesity
- Cramps or muscle spasms
- Erectile dysfunction
- Fainting spells
- Headache
- Heart disease
- Hypertension (high blood pressure)
- Loss of libido
- Lowered immunity
- Muscle aches
- Nail biting
- Nervous twitches
- Pins and needles
- Sleep difficulties
- Stomach upset

Effects on Thoughts and Feelings

- Anger
- Anxiety
- Burnout
- Depression

- Insecurity
- Forgetfulness
- Irritability
- Trouble concentrating
- Restlessness
- Sadness
- Fatigue

Effects on Behavior

- Overeating or undereating
- Food cravings
- Sudden angry outbursts
- Drug abuse
- Alcohol abuse
- Increased tobacco use
- Social withdrawal
- Frequent crying
- Relationship problems

Common Causes of Stress

- Bereavement
- Family problems
- Financial pressure
- Illness
- Job issues / losing a job
- Lack of time
- Moving
- Relationships (including divorce)
- Abortion
- Becoming a parent
- Workplace conflict
- Heavy traffic / difficult driving

- Fear of crime
- Miscarriage
- Overcrowding
- Pollution
- Pregnancy
- Retirement
- Excessive noise
- Uncertainty (waiting for lab results, exams, interviews, etc.)

(The lists of stressors and effects are adapted from medical references such as WebMD.)

That's an amazing list of complications—and they all stem from stress. No wonder so much has been written on it. Before we learn how to conquer stress, it's important to understand **what stress is.**

Stress: *A state of mental or emotional strain or tension resulting from adverse or very demanding circumstances.*

That definition gets us closer. Let's go a little deeper. Simply put, **stress is fear.** Keep an open mind and consider this.

What we commonly call *stress* is the **physical manifestation of fear**—fear's effect on the body. Think about how you feel when you're afraid. Now think about how you feel when you're stressed. Still not convinced? Try swapping the words in everyday sentences:

- "I've been so **stressed** about my health lately."
  → "I've been so **afraid** about my health lately."
- "Bob, I'm **stressed** about getting that report in on time."
  → "Bob, I'm **afraid** I won't get that report in on time."

Other situations are less obvious:

- "My wife is stressing me out."
- "I can't take any more stress at work."
- "These bills are piling up—and so is the stress."

At first glance you might say, *I'm not afraid of my wife, my work, or my bills.* (For the record, you probably should be a little afraid of your wife—kidding!) You may not fear the person or thing itself, but perhaps you fear **not meeting expectations**, **facing discipline or job loss**, or **not having enough to cover the bills**—leading to repossession or bankruptcy.

No one likes to admit fear. The adversary exploits that. If we say we're *afraid*, we worry we'll look weak or incompetent. But if we say we're *stressed*, people understand and even sympathize. Here's the danger: when Satan nudged us to relabel **fear** as **stress**, he altered how we fight it. Scripture clearly teaches how to combat **fear**; search for how to conquer "stress" (as our culture defines it) and you'll find far less clarity. We all experience stress, but we don't fight it effectively because we haven't **named it** correctly.

Name it, and its grip loosens. **Stress is fear.** Now that we know what stress really is, we can pursue the **biblical tools** needed to destroy it.

And I'm not going to leave you hanging—we'll go after those tools in the **next chapter**.

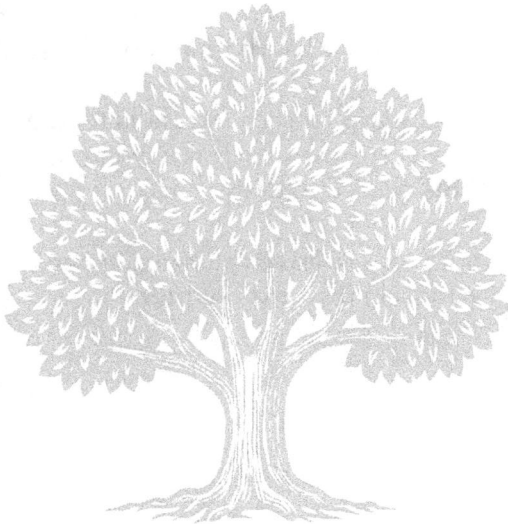

CHAPTER 8
HOW TO OVERCOME FEAR
AND ANXIETY

I think this chapter could just as accurately be titled:
"How to overcome fear, anxiety, stress, alarm, apprehension,
angst, concern, despair, dismay, doubt, dread, horror, jitters,
panic, suspicion, terror, uneasiness, worry, abhorrence,
agitation, aversion, awe, consternation, cowardice, discomposure,
distress, faintheartedness, foreboding, fright, timidity, trembling,
trepidation, chicken-heartedness, cold feet, and the like."

If you just read the last chapter on stress, you may
understand why. If you have not read the previous

chapter, I highly recommend that you do so now; I'll wait…

You're back! All caught up? Good. Let's continue. The devil—our adversary—has done an exemplary job of pulling the proverbial wool over our eyes by redefining what *fear* is. He would have you believe that what you're feeling is anything and everything **but** fear. *It's stress. It's anxiety. It's shyness. It's cold feet. I'm just in a funk.* And he's cultivated an equally impressive collection of (may I be so bold as to say) purposely ineffective remedies for everything but fear. *For example: "If you have anxiety, it's not your fault you can't control how you feel—here, take this pill for the rest of your life."*

I want to pause and say: I have personally struggled with anxiety—not run-of-the-mill anxiety, but debilitating, sweat-inducing, knee-knocking, can't-breathe *this-is-it* anxiety. The kind that makes you think you're going to die of a heart attack, brain aneurysm, and stroke simultaneously, and then find yourself, when it's over, covered in your own vomit. I'm sorry to be crude, but it's no joke. **I had it. I had it bad.** The keyword is **had**; I'll expand upon my experience a little later. For now, back to the point.

Here, take this pill for the rest of your life and be dependent on something other than God. That's Satan's goal—to keep you hopelessly dependent on anything but God. The remedy to fear and anxiety is **hope**. Hope is the antithesis of fear in all its forms.

Find Out What You're Dealing With

For any treatment to be effective, you must first **diagnose** the problem. You can take antibiotics all day long, but they'll do absolutely no good if you have scurvy. (Scurvy, by the way, is a vitamin C deficiency most common among seafarers before the 20th century.) So how do you know what you're dealing with? By taking an **objective** look at your issue. Dissect it. Walk through the emotions involved. Really think about it.

Let's have an example, shall we?

As I mentioned, I used to struggle with anxiety. Before that, as a child, I struggled with horrible nightmares. This will become relevant in a moment. The world closely associates fear and anxiety, but it doesn't consider them exactly the same. My struggle with anxiety started in my late teens and continued well into my late twenties before I was able to get it under control.

I believed what the world told me: *It's not your fault. There's nothing you can do to control it. It's out of your hands. The only hope you have is this little pill. Sure, you can think positively and do breathing exercises, but it's brain chemistry. It's just how you're made. It's no big deal.*

It wasn't until I began to build my relationship with Jesus Christ that I saw how big a lie that was. The closer I grew to Jesus, the more I saw through the enemy's tactics. It didn't happen overnight—it took time. Eventually, I **identified my fear**: uncertainty about my salvation. I was afraid of death—afraid of dying, afraid of where I'd spend eternity. And the devil knew it; he exploited it. He battered me for years with what the world calls clinical anxiety/panic disorder.

For those interested, here is a summary of those symptoms:

Clinical anxiety/panic disorder differs from normal fear and anxiety responses to stressful events. Panic disorder is a serious condition that can strike without reason or warning. Symptoms include sudden attacks of fear and nervousness, with physical symptoms such as sweating and a racing heart. During a panic attack, the fear response is out of proportion to the situation, which often is not threatening. Over time, a constant fear of another attack can affect daily functioning and quality of life. Panic attacks (often lasting about 10 minutes) may include difficulty breathing, pounding heart or chest pain, intense dread, choking or smothering sensation, dizziness or faintness, trembling or shaking, sweating, nausea or stomachache, tingling or numbness in fingers and toes, chills or hot flashes, and a fear of losing control or dying.
(Adapted from medical references such as WebMD.)

Sounds appealing, doesn't it? I was quite literally tortured—and many of you have been too.

Nightmares, Sleep Paralysis, and the Name of Jesus

This is where my childhood nightmares come into play. Long before the anxiety began, I had the most horrible dreams—disgusting, awful dreams of being tortured by what I knew, even then, to be demons. The settings varied, but the content was the same:

anywhere from twenty to a hundred distorted figures grasping and fighting over me, pulling at every limb. I would scream and plead for my mother, but my screams were silent. I'd wake up sweaty and terrified and run to my parents' room. Sometimes I was met with frustration and sent back to bed. Thank God, most of the time I was greeted with a calm voice in the dark.

My mother was a young Christian. She would pray with me—that's all she knew to do. Eventually she told me to **call on the name of Jesus**. I didn't fully understand when she said He loved me and died for my sins. All I knew was that when I was scared, I could call on Him. So I did. The next time I woke from a nightmare, I whispered, "Jesus… Jesus… Jesus."

The nightmares continued, but I found comfort in calling on His name, even as I still ran to my parents' bedroom. Relief finally came when my aunt visited. She asked me about my dreams and what I thought was attacking me, then led me in prayer. At the end she had me ask for protection. I asked God to **put a bubble around my bed** so nothing bad could get me while I slept. That night was the first in a long time without a bad dream. That became my routine: my mother would pray with me, and I would ask God for that "bubble."

I prayed that prayer nightly until my early teens. I spent my childhood and adolescence in church and began growing a personal relationship with my Savior. I happily attended services three times a week. I even asked to be baptized during a Royal Rangers retreat in the Shenandoah Mountains—overwhelmed by a waterfall's beauty, I asked my leader to baptize me right there.

Around age thirteen we moved, and I lost connection with that church. Through a series of events I won't detail here, I took my focus off God. The further I walked from Him, the further I walked from His protection. While I walked with Christ, He covered me; His grace guarded me; His promises applied to me; my hope was in Him. God's gifts are **conditional**—they apply while you actively have a personal relationship with His Son Jesus. His promises are directly connected to Jesus. Walk away from Him and you walk away from His promises.

Shortly after, the dreams returned with a vengeance. I also began to experience **sleep paralysis**—waking from a nightmare unable to move, only my eyes functioning, even my breathing feeling beyond my control, with the same oppressive presence in the room.

Sleep paralysis is a phenomenon in which, when falling asleep or awakening, a person temporarily cannot move, speak, or react. It's a transitional state between wakefulness and sleep, marked by muscle atonia. It's often accompanied by terrifying hallucinations (e.g., an intruder in the room) and physical sensations (e.g., a strong current through the body). One hypothesis is disrupted REM sleep. It has been linked to narcolepsy, migraines, anxiety disorders, and obstructive sleep apnea; it can also occur in isolation.
(Adapted from medical references such as WebMD.)

Science can **describe** aspects of the experience; unless you've lived it, you don't know how terrifying it is.

There I was—paralyzed, terrified, watching something approach. I couldn't get up. My mind raced, adrenaline surged. Then it clicked: **Call on the name of Jesus.** I tried to form the word but couldn't. I cried it out in my mind. Seconds felt like eternity. I tried again—managed to move my lip, but no air. I kept trying, closer each time. My voice, to my ears, was faint and distorted. By God's grace, the word finally came together and I **whispered, "Jesus."** In that instant, two things happened: the malevolent force was gone, and I was set free. I regained full control—movement, breathing, speech. I said "Jesus" again as I ran to the light switch. That wasn't my last attack or nightmare. It took years. I drifted into a comfortable balance of religion and worldliness— right where the adversary wanted me.

Naming the Root—and Rebuilding Faith

I share all of this to explain how I overcame. I thought I knew what the Bible said about fear, and I thought I believed it. You can imagine my frustration when I tried to apply Scripture and still felt afraid. It wasn't until I examined **why** these things scared me so much that I found the root. My internal Q&A went like this:

- *When my panic attack is strongest, how do I feel?* **I'm afraid.**

- *What am I afraid of?*
  Dying.
- *Why am I afraid of dying?*
  Because I don't know where I'm going, and I don't want to go to hell.
- *Why don't I know where I'll spend eternity?*
  Because…I'm afraid I'm not saved.

Boom. There it was. The Scriptures I tried to apply had no effect because I didn't have **faith.** I couldn't accept God's promises because I didn't believe they applied to me. I couldn't receive His protection because I had walked too far from Him. I fell into a common trap: trying to live a dual life—one foot in the world, one foot with God.

I still had a dilemma: *How can I believe something I don't understand?* My answer was in:

Matthew 18:2–4 – *"And calling to Him a child, He put him in the midst of them and said, 'Truly, I say to you, unless you turn and become like children, you will never enter the kingdom of heaven. Whoever humbles himself like this child is the greatest in the kingdom of heaven.'"*

I had to return to the faith I had when I was seven—asking God to put a bubble around my bed. I didn't need to understand **how** He would do it; I needed to **believe** He would. I had to return to the faith of that preteen boy who saw God's hand in mountains and waterfalls. You can't stay in blind childlike faith forever; it's dangerous to remain immature. But every person's faith must start somewhere, and that's where mine began to **grow.**

Ephesians 2:8–9 – *"For by grace you have been saved through faith. And this is not your own doing; it is the gift of God, not a result of works, so that no one may boast."*
Romans 10:17 – *"So then faith comes by hearing, and hearing by the word of God."* (KJV)

It didn't take long to reconfirm my salvation and see my faith grow. That didn't immediately end the attacks—though the nightmares faded quickly. The panic attacks lingered, but with each one, God was with me, and each attack was less effective than the last. Eventually I found myself praying **in the middle** of a panic attack:

"Father, if it's my time to go, take me. To be absent from the body is to be present with the Lord. I love You, and I trust You."

Boom—again. I finally got it. There's nothing that can happen to me that my God cannot see me through. God doesn't promise we won't face trials, but He **does** promise to be with us in them. That's our security. When you trust God with your very life and well-being, it doesn't matter what you face, because you know He loves you and holds your best interests at the forefront.

Psalm 23:4 (KJV) – *"Yea, though I walk through the valley of the shadow of death, I will fear no evil: for Thou art with me; Thy rod and Thy staff they comfort me."*
Lamentations 3:37–38 – *"Who is there who speaks and it comes to pass unless the Lord has commanded it? Is it not from the mouth of the Most High that both good and ill go forth?"*

Let me put it this way: I'd rather be **in the fiery furnace** knowing God is with me than walking on a beach living the dream **without** Him. I've become 100% dependent on Him. I've put my faith in people and been let down; in myself and fallen short; in the world and watched it erode. Only God never fails. He alone can keep **all** His promises.

Matthew 10:28 – *"And do not fear those who kill the body but cannot kill the soul. Rather fear Him who can destroy both soul and body in hell."*

There's nothing the adversary can do that has any eternal effect on a believer. It may be uncomfortable—even painful. So what? If you think the Christian life is easy, free of persecution and pain, and always financially prosperous, you're believing a lie. Stop looking for your reward here on earth; you won't find it here.

Learn from Job (Please Actually Read It)

What can we expect? Look at **Job**. As a matter of fact, take time to read it now. I'm serious—go get your Bible and read. You'll gain far more than you will from the summarized children's version I'm about to quote for those who refuse to read it themselves.

If you're still reading, you're either (A) done with Job—welcome back—or (B) stubborn. If it's B, consider adjusting your attitude toward instruction.

Proverbs 13:18 – *"Poverty and shame will come to him who refuses instruction, but he who heeds rebuke will be honored."*

Proverbs 12:1 – *"Whoever loves instruction loves knowledge, but he who hates correction is stupid."* (plain translation)
Hosea 4:6 – *"My people are destroyed for lack of knowledge; because you have rejected knowledge, I also will reject you."*

It's important to have a **teachable** spirit. In love, not rudeness: if you didn't read Job, ask yourself why. We're here to learn, and learning requires openness to instruction.

Without further delay, here's the **story of Job** (Oh, by the way this, version just so happens to be out of a children's book called The Children's Bible by Henry A. Sherman and Charles Foster Kent. Enjoy!):

/In the land of Uz there lived a man named **Job**; and he was blameless and upright, one who revered God and avoided evil. He had seven sons and three daughters. He owned seven thousand sheep, three thousand camels, five hundred yoke of oxen, five hundred asses; and he had many servants, so that he was the richest man among all the peoples of the East.

One day when the sons of God came before **Jehovah**, **Satan** came with them. Jehovah said to Satan, "From where do you come?" Satan answered, "From going back and forth on the earth, and walking up and down on it." And Jehovah said to Satan,

"Have you seen my servant Job? For there is no man like him on the earth—blameless and upright, who reveres God and avoids evil."

Satan answered, "But is it for nothing that Job reveres God? Have you not yourself made a hedge all about him, about his household, and about all that he has? You have blessed whatever he does, and his possessions have greatly increased. But just put out your hand now and take away all he has; he certainly will curse you to your face."

Then Jehovah said to Satan, "See, everything that he has is in your power; only do not lay hands on Job himself." So Satan left the presence of Jehovah.

One day, as Job's sons and daughters were eating and drinking in the oldest brother's house, a messenger came to Job and said, "The oxen were **plowing** and the asses were grazing near them when Sabeans suddenly attacked and seized them; the servants were put to the sword, and I alone have escaped to tell you."

While he was still speaking, another messenger came and said, "Lightning has fallen from heaven and has completely burned up the sheep and the servants, and I alone have escaped to tell you."

While this man was still speaking, another messenger came and said, "The Chaldeans, attacking in three bands, raided the camels and drove them away; the servants were put to the sword, and I alone have escaped to tell you."

While this one was still speaking, another messenger came and said, "Your sons and daughters were eating and drinking in their oldest brother's house when a great wind came from across the wilderness, struck the four corners of the house, and it fell upon the young men and killed them. I alone have escaped to tell you."

Then Job rose, tore his robe, shaved his head, threw himself on the ground, and worshiped, saying:
"Jehovah gave, Jehovah has taken away;
Blessed be the name of Jehovah!"
In all this Job did not sin nor blame God.

On another day when the sons of God came before Jehovah, Satan came with them. And Jehovah said to Satan, "From where do you come?" Satan answered, "From going back and forth on the earth, and from walking up and down on it." Jehovah said to Satan, "Have you seen my servant Job? For there is no man like him on the earth—blameless and upright, one who reveres God and avoids evil; he still is faithful, although you led me to ruin him without **cause**."
Satan answered Jehovah, "Skin for skin—yes, a man will give all that he has for his life. But just put out your hand now, and touch his bone and his flesh; he certainly will curse you to your face."
Jehovah said to Satan, "See, he is in your power; only spare his life."

So Satan left the presence of Jehovah and afflicted Job from the sole of his foot to the crown of his head with leprosy so terrible that Job took a piece of broken pottery with which to scrape himself. As he sat among the ashes, his wife said to him, "Are you still holding to your piety? Curse God and die."
But he said to her, "You speak like a senseless woman. We accept prosperity from God; shall we not

also accept misfortune?" In all this Job said nothing
that was wrong.

When Job's three friends heard of all this trouble that
had befallen him, they came each from his own
home—**Eliphaz the Temanite**, **Bildad the Shuhite**,
and **Zophar the Naamathite**—for they had arranged
to go together to show their sympathy for him and
comfort him. But when they saw him in the distance,
they did not at first know him. Then they all wept
aloud and tore their robes and threw dust upon their
heads. And they sat down with him on the ground
seven days and seven nights without anyone saying a
word to him, for they saw that he was in great
trouble.

Then Job began to speak and said:
"Why did I not die at birth,
Breathe my last when I was born?
I should then have lain down in quiet,
Should have slept and been at rest
With kings and **counselors** of earth,
Who built themselves great pyramids;
With princes rich in gold,
Who filled their houses with silver.
There the wicked cease from troubling,
There the weary are at rest;
Captives too at ease together,
Hearing not the voice of masters.
There the small and great are gathered,
There the slave is free at last."

Then **Eliphaz**, the Temanite, answered:
"If one dares to speak, will it vex you?

But who can keep from speaking?
See! you have instructed many,
And strengthened the drooping hands.
Your words have upheld the fallen,
Giving strength to tottering knees.
But now that trouble comes, you are impatient,
Now that it touches you, you lose courage.
Is not your religion your confidence;
Your blameless life, your hope?
Remember! What innocent man ever perished?
Or where were the upright ever destroyed?
Happy the man whom God corrects;
Therefore, spurn not the Almighty's chastening.
For he causes pain but to comfort,
And wounds, that his hands may heal."

Then **Job** answered:
"What strength have I, that I should endure?
And what is my future, that I should be patient?
Is my strength the strength of stones,
Or is my body made of brass?
A friend should be kind to one fainting,
Though he lose his faith in the Almighty.
Teach me, and I will keep silent.
Show me how I have sinned."

Then **Bildad**, the Shuhite, answered:
"Is God a God of injustice?
Or can the Almighty do wrong?
If your children sinned against him,
He has let them suffer the penalty;
But you should earnestly seek him,
And devoutly beseech the Almighty.
If you are pure and upright,

He will surely answer your prayer,
And will prosper your righteous abode."

Then **Job** answered:
"To be sure, I know that it is so;
But how can a man be just before God?
He is wise in mind and mighty in strength—
Who has ever defied him and prospered?
Blameless I am! I regard not myself;
I hate my life; it is all one to me.
Therefore, I openly declare:
He destroys the blameless as well as the wicked."

Then **Zophar**, the Naamathite, answered:
"If you would cleanse your heart,
And stretch out your hands to God,
And put away sin from your hand,
And let no wrong dwell in your tent,
You would then lift your face without spot,
You would then be steadfast and fearless."

Then **Job** answered:
"Verily you are the people,
And with you wisdom shall die!
But I have a mind as well as you,
And who does not know all this?
Oh, that my words were now written,
That they were inscribed in a book,
That with an iron pen and with lead
In rock they were carved forever!
For I know that my Defender lives,
That at last he shall stand upon earth;
And after this skin is destroyed,
Freed from my flesh, I shall see him,

Whom I shall behold for myself;
My own eyes shall see, and no stranger's."

Job again spoke and said:
"Oh, to be as in months of old,
As in days when God guarded my steps,
When his lamp shone above my head,
And I walked by his light through the darkness;
As I was in my prosperous days,
When God protected my tent;
When still the Almighty was with me,
And my children were all about me!
When I went to the gate of the city,
And took my seat in the open,
The youths, when they saw me, retired,
And the aged rose up and stood;
The princes refrained from talking,
And laid their hands on their mouths;
The voices of nobles were hushed,
And their tongues stuck fast to their palates.
He who heard of me called me happy,
He who saw me bore me witness,
For I saved the poor who cried,
And the orphan with none to help him.
The suffering gave me their blessing,
And I made the widow's heart glad.
Eyes was I to the blind,
Feet was I to the lame,
And a father to those who were needy.
I defended the cause of the stranger,
I shattered the jaws of the wicked,
And wrested the prey from his teeth.
Men listened to me eagerly,
And in silence awaited my counsel.

After my words they spoke not,
And my speech fell as **raindrops** upon them.
But they sing of me now in derision,
And my name is a byword among them.
Oh, for someone to hear me!
Behold my defense all signed!
Let now the Almighty answer,
Let Jehovah write the charge!
On my shoulder I would bear it,
As a crown I would bind it round me;
I would tell him my every act;
Like a prince I would enter his presence!"

Then, **out of the whirlwind**, Jehovah answered Job:
"Where were you when I founded the earth?
You have knowledge and insight, so tell me.
You must know! Who determined its measures?
Or who measured it off with a line?
On what were its foundations placed?
Or who laid its cornerstone,
When the morning stars all sang together,
And the sons of God shouted for joy?
Can you lift up your voice to the clouds,
That abundance of water may answer you?
Can you send on their missions the lightnings;
To you do they say, 'Here we are'?
Does the hawk soar because of your wisdom,
And stretch her wings to the south wind?
Does the eagle mount up at your bidding,
And build her nest on high?
Will the fault-finder strive with Almighty?
He who argues with God, let him answer.
Will you set aside my judgment,
And condemn me, that you may be justified?"

Then Job answered **the Lord**:
"How small I am! What can I answer?
I lay my hand on my mouth.
I spoke once, but will do so no more;
Yes, twice, but will go no further.
I know thou canst do all things,
And that nothing with thee is impossible.
I spoke, therefore, without sense,
Of wonders beyond my knowledge.
I had heard of thee but by hearsay,
But now my eye has seen thee;
Therefore, I despise my words,
And repent in dust and ashes."

Then Jehovah gave back to Job **twice** as much as he had before. And Jehovah blessed the last part of Job's life more than the first; and he had fourteen thousand sheep, six thousand camels, a thousand yoke of oxen, and a thousand asses. He also had seven sons and three daughters. And after this Job lived **a** hundred and forty years.

What did we learn?

- Job loved God.
- God blessed Job.
- Satan claimed Job loved God only because of blessing.
- God allowed Satan to take away Job's blessings.
- Job continued to praise God regardless of circumstances.
- God was proven right.
- God restored Job's blessings.

Many scholars believe Job was a real person who endured these events.

Satan stands as **accuser of the brethren:**

Revelation 12:10 – *"...for the accuser of our brothers has been thrown down, who accuses them day and night before our God."*

This life isn't easy. It's hard, unfair, painful, unforgiving—because of sin. Your reward is not here; it's in **heaven.**

The Answer: Blood and Testimony

I could have told you earlier, but you might not have grasped it. Here is the answer to how to overcome fear and anxiety:

By the blood of the Lamb and by the word of your testimony.
(cf. Revelation 12:11)

Those aren't churchy slogans; they're **weapons.** Let's unpack both—and then put them to work.

1) "The Blood of the Lamb" — What It Means and How to Stand in It

What it means.
Jesus' blood is the **objective basis** of your peace. His

atoning death satisfies God's justice, removes your guilt, disarms the accuser, and secures your adoption. That's why believers can say, "I am safe," even when their feelings scream otherwise.

- *Forgiveness secured:* "In Him we have redemption **through His blood**, the forgiveness of sins" (Eph. 1:7).
- *Accusations silenced:* The enemy's case collapses where the blood has been applied (cf. Rom. 8:33–34).
- *Peace established:* "Since we have been justified by faith, we have **peace with God** through our Lord Jesus Christ" (Rom. 5:1).

How to stand in it (practically).

1. **Confess and agree with God.** Name sin plainly; don't bargain with it (1 John 1:7–9). Clean conscience, quieter fears.
2. **Thank God out loud for the cross.** Anxiety often shouts; thanksgiving resets the soul (Col. 2:13–15; Phil. 4:6–7).
3. **Refuse the accuser's voice.** When condemnation rises, answer it: *"I have an advocate with the Father—Jesus Christ the righteous"* (1 John 2:1).
4. **Anchor identity in redemption, not performance.** "You were **bought with a price**" (1 Cor. 6:20). Your worth and safety are not self-managed.

Think of it this way: the blood is **God's receipt**—paid in full. When fear waves a past-due notice, you hold up the receipt.

2) "The Word of Your Testimony" — What It Is and How to Use It

What it is.
Your testimony is your **lived history with God**—the concrete ways He has met you, kept you, carried you, corrected you, protected you. It is truth you have proven in the trenches, not theories you admire from a distance.

- *Biblical pattern:* David didn't face Goliath with ideas; he faced him with testimony: "The LORD who delivered me from the paw of the lion… **will deliver me** from the hand of this Philistine" (1 Sam. 17:37).

How to use it (practically).

1. **Write it down in scenes.** Note the problem, the promise you leaned on, what you prayed, and how God answered. Keep a short "Deliverance Log."
2. **Speak it back to your soul.** "Why are you cast down, O my soul?… **Hope in God**" (Ps. 42:5). Your mouth can preach your heart into peace.
3. **Aim it at the lie.** If the lie is *"God won't come through this time,"* answer with *your* record of His faithfulness.

4. **Share it.** Testimony feeds others' faith and reinforces your own (2 Cor. 1:3–4).

Your testimony turns yesterday's battles into **today's ammunition**.

Faith and Hope—How They Work Together

- **Hope** looks forward with *confident expectation* because of what Jesus has done.
- **Faith** steps forward with *obedient action* because hope is real.

"Faith is the **assurance** of things **hoped for**" (Heb. 11:1). Hope fills the tank; faith presses the pedal.

When the Attack Feels Demonic

I believe my condition was, in hindsight, a **demonic attack**. Scripture says our struggle is not merely "flesh and blood" (Eph. 6:12). If you sense that sharp, oppressive, lying pressure:

1. **Stand under the blood (position).** *"I belong to Jesus; I am covered, forgiven, and sealed by His Spirit."*
2. **Resist with Scripture (precision).** Answer the specific lie with a specific verse (Matt. 4:1–11).
3. **Command and refuse (authority).** *"In Jesus' name, I renounce fear and every lying spirit. Leave now."* (Luke 10:19; James 4:7)

4. **Invite praise and light (presence).**
   Darkness hates worship (Ps. 22:3). Put on
   worship music; read Scripture aloud.
5. **Lock arms (people).** Ask trusted believers to
   pray with you (Eccl. 4:12).

This isn't theatrics; it's **standing** in what Christ
already won.

**A Simple "Blood & Testimony" Prayer You Can
Pray: Father,** I thank You for the **blood of Jesus.** By
His blood I am forgiven, cleansed, and adopted.
There is no condemnation for me in Christ.
Lord Jesus, You are my peace. You purchased me; I
am Yours.
Holy Spirit, bear witness with my spirit that I am a
child of God. Fill my heart with Your love and drive
out fear.
I **renounce** the lie that I am unsafe, alone, or beyond
help. I **receive** Your truth: You are with me, You are
for me, and You will never leave me.
What You have done for me before, You will do
again. **You delivered me when [name a past
moment].** I testify to Your faithfulness.
In the **name of Jesus,** I resist fear and every lying
spirit. **Go,** and do not return.
I set my hope fully on the grace that is mine in Christ.
Amen.

Pray it slowly. Mean it. Repeat it when the waves rise.

Daily "Overcome" Rhythm (Quick Start)

- **Morning — Covering:** Read a short passage (Psalm 27; Romans 8; John 14). Thank God for the cross.
- **Midday — Testify:** Rehearse one line of testimony: *"God met me when..."*
- **Evening — Examen:** Note where fear tried to speak and where God was faithful. End with gratitude (Phil. 4:6–7).
- **Always — Community:** Text a friend: *"Stand with me; here's what I'm resisting and what I'm declaring."*

Two Guardrails

- This is **not** magic language. The power is Jesus Himself, not our phrasing.
- Use **wisdom** too. Rest, boundaries, peacemaking conversations, and—when needed—competent Christian counseling can be part of God's provision. None of that replaces the cross; it **applies** its benefits to your whole life.

Bottom Line

The **blood of the Lamb** settles your standing with God. The **word of your testimony** settles your heart in that truth when the storm hits. Live under the blood; fight with your testimony. If you position yourself to be **dependent** on God's promises and put your **hope** in Jesus the Messiah, you will, in time, find you have **nothing left to fear**.

CHAPTER 9
HOW TO HANDLE
YOUR FINANCES

The he Bible isn't shy about money. In fact, it has a lot to say. So why so much confusion? As Christians, we should handle finances the same way we handle everything else—**by applying God's Word**.

Because Scripture says so much on this topic, let's break it into three categories:

- **Tithes & Offerings**
- **Debt**
- **Stewardship**

Tithes & Offerings

Tithing is often discussed from two angles—**Old Testament** and **New Testament**.

Old Testament Tithing

Some churches teach that you must give **10%** of your income based on Old Testament commands:

Leviticus 27:30 – "Every tithe of the land, whether of the seed of the land or of the fruit of the trees, is the LORD's; it is holy to the LORD."
Numbers 18:26 – "Moreover, you shall speak and say to the Levites, 'When you take from the people of Israel the tithe... then you shall present a contribution from it to the LORD, a tithe of the tithe.'"
Deuteronomy 14:24 – "And if the way is too long for you, so that you are not able to carry the tithe..."
2 Chronicles 31:5 – "As soon as the command was spread abroad, the people of Israel gave in abundance the firstfruits... and they brought in abundantly the tithe of everything."

"Tithe" literally means **a tenth**. The pattern also appears earlier:

Genesis 28:20–22 – *Jacob vowed* "...of all that You give me I will give a **full tenth** to You."

It's easy to see why a fixed 10% appeals to church operations: predictable generosity funds ministry, benevolence, and logistics. Still, many churches today emphasize the **New Testament** approach.

New Testament Giving

Leaders often **recommend** 10% as a wise starting point—*not* a law. The New Testament does not command a percentage; it emphasizes **heart posture**:

2 Corinthians 9:7 – "Each one must give **as he has decided in his heart**, not reluctantly or under compulsion, for God loves a **cheerful giver**."
1 Corinthians 16:2 – "On the first day of every week, each of you is to put something aside… **as he may prosper**…"

The key difference is **motive**. We don't give to avoid punishment; we give because **He first loved us**. Jesus' teaching pushes generosity **beyond a minimum**:

Luke 12:33 – "Sell your possessions, and give to the needy… with a treasure in the heavens that does not fail."
Luke 21:1–4 – *The Widow's Offering*: she gave "**all she had to live on**."

Her faith wasn't in two copper coins but in **God's provision**. That's the kind of dependence the New Testament commends.

Where to give? Traditionally, we give to the **local church**—our "storehouse"—because elders and leaders are positioned to **identify needs** and **distribute** wisely (benevolence, food ministries, missions, operations). But the New Covenant also urges **Spirit-led** generosity: give as much as you can, as often as you can, **to whom the Lord leads**. Give joyfully, not for show or from selfish ambition.

Larry Burkett put it well in *Giving and Tithing*:

"The New Testament talks about the importance and benefits of giving. We are to give **as we are able**... Sometimes more than 10 percent; sometimes less... Every Christian should diligently pray and seek God's wisdom... Above all... with **pure motives** and an **attitude of worship**... 'Each man should give what he has decided in his heart... for God loves a cheerful giver' (2 Corinthians 9:7)."

Bottom line: In Christ, the question isn't "How little can I give?" but **"Lord, how much would You have me give, and where?"**

Debt

Debt is a modern epidemic. (Years ago CNN reported average U.S. credit-card balances in the many thousands—**before** mortgages, car notes, or student loans.) The issue has bled into Christian homes and churches. Often we reach outside our means not because we **must**, but because we're **unsatisfied** with what we have—or because life hit hard and we relied on convenience.

Sometimes we spend to soothe emotions, to "keep up," or to feel secure. Sometimes genuine needs arise—medical bills, broken cars, job loss. However it happens, the end is the same: **debt**.

What Scripture Says

The Bible doesn't outright forbid borrowing, but it gives **strong cautions**:

Romans 13:8 – "**Owe no one anything**, except to love each other…"
Proverbs 22:7 – "The rich rules over the poor, and the **borrower is slave** of the lender."
Hebrews 13:5 – "Keep your life free from **love of money**, and be content with what you have…"

Debt can be a heavy yoke. Reserve it for **rare, necessary** situations—and bring every major purchase before God in prayer. Ask, *"Do I need this, or am I feeding discontent?"* Paul learned contentment in **every** circumstance (Philippians 4:10–13). That is the antidote to compulsive spending.

Mary Hunt (*Debt-Proof Living*) offers wise, biblical counsel:

"The Bible neither expressly forbids nor condones borrowing… it is **usually not a good idea**… Debt essentially makes us a slave to the lender. In some cases it may be a 'necessary evil'—**if** handled wisely and payments are manageable."

When you're already in over your head:

1. **Pray for wisdom** (James 1:5). Fight anxiety with prayer and thanksgiving (Philippians 4:6).
2. **Cut lifestyle costs** to bare minimums. Eliminate non-essentials.
3. **Build a real budget** from *actual* income and *actual* expenses—and **follow it**.
4. **Give intentionally** (2 Corinthians 9:7). Honor God with a prayerful, cheerful plan.
5. **Seek counsel** (pastor, biblical financial coach; ministries like Crown).
6. **Call creditors** to negotiate rates and payments. Ask for mercy and structure.
7. **Discipline your habits.** Cut the cards if needed. Recruit an accountability partner.
8. **Start now.** Small faithful steps, month after month, break bondage.

Bottom line: Debt isn't unforgivable—it's **addressable**. But wisdom says: avoid it whenever possible, and **pursue contentment**.

Stewardship

We are **stewards**—not owners.

John 3:27 – "A person cannot receive even one thing unless it is given him from heaven."
1 Peter 4:10 – "As each has received a gift, **use it to serve one another**, as good stewards of God's varied grace."

Because what we have is **entrusted**, not possessed, we spend and save with **God's purposes** in view: caring for the poor and needy, resourcing the local church, providing for our households, and enjoying God's gifts **within His boundaries**. Think back to the "fenced yard": inside the fence of God's moral will, there's freedom. Stewardship is learning to walk that yard well—**listening** for the Spirit's guidance and applying biblical principles.

The Parable of the Talents (Matthew 25:14–30)

"It will be like a man going on a journey, who called his servants and entrusted to them his property…" *(read full passage)*

Notice: the master expected **increase**, not mere preservation. The third servant buried his talent out of **fear**—and was rebuked as "wicked and slothful." Stewardship is not hoarding; it's **faithful, wise, fruitful** management. Like those servants, we will give an account for how we handled what God placed in our hands—**time, abilities, resources, and money**.

Marks of a Faithful Steward

- **Worshipful giving** (cheerful, God-directed).
- **Contented living** (gratitude, not grasping).
- **Honest budgeting** (clarity + obedience).
- **Wise saving** (ant-like prudence without fear-driven hoarding).
- **Purposeful investing** (seeking fruitfulness that honors God and helps others).
- **Regular accountability** (inviting counsel and correction).

Putting It All Together: A Simple Plan

1. **Pray first.** "Lord, it's all Yours—lead me."
2. **Decide your giving** (start somewhere concrete, grow from there, and follow the Spirit).
3. **Make a zero-based budget** (every dollar named; track for 90 days).
4. **Build a small emergency fund** (even $500–$1,000 changes emergencies into inconveniences).
5. **Attack high-interest debt** (negotiate rates; pay down with intensity).
6. **Live simply.** Choose contentment over comparison; delay wants.
7. **Review monthly** with a spouse/accountability partner; adjust as the Spirit leads.

Final Word

Money is a discipleship issue before it's a math issue. Budgets and spreadsheets matter, but they only reveal the heart that's steering them (Matthew 6:21). Before we ask, "Can I afford this?" we ask, "**Does this honor Jesus?**" When Christ is Lord over our wallets, He is Lord over our wants, our worries, and our plans.

Give from love. We don't give to pay God back or to earn favor—we give because **He first loved us** and gave Himself for us. Cheerful, Spirit-led generosity trains our hearts to trust God more than money (2 Corinthians 9:7). Start with a concrete, prayed-through plan, then stay open to Holy Spirit nudges—needs in your church, a missionary, a neighbor. Generosity is worship in motion.

Borrow rarely. Scripture doesn't outlaw lending, but it **warns** us: debt puts us under a yoke (Proverbs 22:7). Use credit only when wisdom and necessity align, not to feed comparison, convenience, or impulse. If you must borrow, do it with counsel, clarity, and a repayment plan that preserves integrity and peace. Freedom today is worth more than upgrades tomorrow.

Steward faithfully. You are a manager, not an owner (1 Peter 4:10). Faithful stewardship is less about guarding piles and more about **growing** what God entrusts—serving people, resourcing the gospel, providing for your household, and planning with prudence (Matthew 25:14–30). Track your spending, tell every dollar where to go, and review regularly with someone who will tell you the truth in love.

When Jesus is the treasure, money finds its place. Christ reorders our desires so that money becomes a **tool:**

- to **bless others** (meeting needs with joy),
- to **fuel the gospel** (supporting your local church and missions),
- to **honor God** (handling resources with integrity, contentment, and gratitude).

A Simple Rule of Thumb

1. **Worship first** — "Lord, it's all Yours."
2. **Give gladly** — decide, then obey with joy.
3. **Live simply** — contentment over comparison.
4. **Save wisely** — margin for storms and opportunities.
5. **Spend intentionally** — every purchase has a purpose.

A Short Prayer

Father, all I have is from Your hand. Teach me to love You more than money, to give with joy, to borrow with caution, and to steward with faith. Make Jesus my treasure so my finances tell the truth about Your worth. **Amen.**

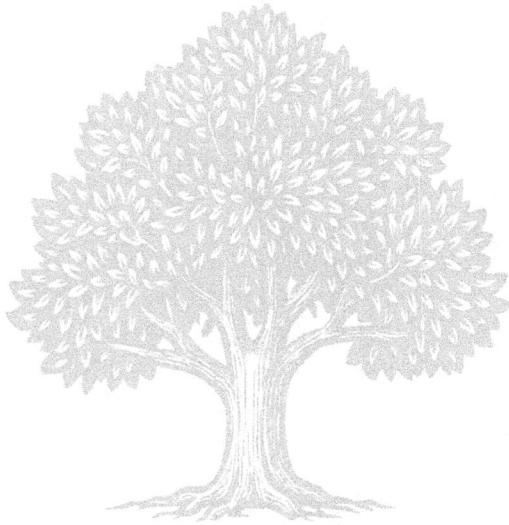

CHAPTER 10
HOW TO OVERCOME GRIEF

If someone you love deeply has recently passed away, I am truly sorry for your loss. I, like you, have experienced the death of a close family member. And maybe—**just maybe**—now is *not* the time for you to read this chapter. That may sound counterintuitive, but what follows might be too much for the rawest moments of sorrow.

Right now, the most important thing to do is **grieve**, not to "overcome" grief. Grieving is a **process**, and processes take **time**. So take time to remember your loved one. Remember the joy of their life. Be with people who love you. And please—**don't forget to cry**. Tears are part of the body's God-given way of releasing pain. So is prayer. If your loved one was a believer, take comfort knowing they are no longer in pain and are joyfully awaiting reunion in Heaven.

One more thought: grief is natural and follows a natural course. But natural grief does not mean giving up on life. When you're ready, come back and finish this chapter. Until then, will you pray with me? And if you're not praying for yourself, would you lift up other readers who are hurting?

"Father, I pray for my dear one who has experienced such a painful loss. Please send Your angels to be with them today—to tend and minister to Your child. Let them feel the warmth of Your love surrounding them in this moment. Keep Your promise never to leave us nor forsake us. Place a soothing balm upon our aching hearts. Father God, we love You, and we ask these things in Jesus' name. Amen."

What Grief Is—and Why It Exists

In an ideal world none of us would ever experience grief. In fact, it was never God's desire for us to suffer it. Grief—like so many other sorrows—is the result of **original sin** (Adam and Eve's disobedience in Eden). Yet, as always, **God has a plan**: He will eradicate sin—and with it, grief—forever.

We usually associate grief with the death of a loved one, but we can also grieve the loss of any significant person, place, or thing. (For example, some people form deep attachments to objects or seasons of life; their loss can ache more than others might expect.) How we handle these losses shapes our future relationships—with people, and most importantly, with **God**.

Grief is an **emotional response to loss**. It should be *proportional* to the value we place on what was lost, and it is **uniquely personal**—we do not all grieve in the same way.

A Hard Truth, Spoken Gently

Here comes an unpopular angle. Often, at the core, grief exposes a kind of **self-concern**: not cruelty or vanity, but the ache that *we* no longer have access to the one we love. We fear that the joy they brought us is gone forever. In our tears, whom are we crying for? In part, **ourselves**. That isn't a condemnation; it's a light in a dark room. To heal, we must bring our pain into the open where God can meet it.

Please hear me: **grieving is not sin**. Job tore his clothes, shaved his head, and wept bitterly—and "**did not sin**" (cf. Job 1:20–22). Grief becomes sinful **only** when, after a season, we refuse God's comfort, grow hard toward His sovereignty, or turn to idols to numb the pain.

Some unhealthy paths look like this:

- Staying **angry at God**, closing your heart to Him.
- **Idolizing** the past—preserving rooms or belongings for years as if time could be frozen.
- Self-medicating with **alcohol, drugs, or compulsions** to avoid feeling.

Because grief is personal, we cannot list every unhealthy pattern—but we can name **healthy** ones.

Healthy Ways to Grieve

1) Receive God's Comfort

Psalm 147:3 – "He heals the brokenhearted and binds up their wounds."
Isaiah 40:1 – "Comfort, yes, comfort My people! says your God."
Matthew 5:4 – "Blessed are those who mourn, for they shall be comforted."
Matthew 11:28 – "Come to Me, all who labor and are heavy laden, and I will give you rest."
Romans 15:4 – "…that through the patience and comfort of the Scriptures we might have hope."
2 Corinthians 1:3 – "The Father of mercies and God of all comfort."

God's comfort is unlike anything else. But He rarely forces it on closed hearts. **Ask** for it. **Expect** it. Sit quietly with Scripture and let Him tend you.

2) Feel What You Feel

In the early days, emotions can collide. Don't suppress them. Numbing may feel easier, but unprocessed sorrow **leaks** into your future. Name feelings as they rise and bring each one to God.

3) Accept Your Limits

Part of healing is acknowledging: *"My loved one is gone, and I cannot change it."* Acceptance isn't betrayal; it's the first door to peace. If you could have reversed this, you would have by now.

4) Set Small, Realistic Goals

The first weeks are hardest. Life feels paused, but bills still come and bodies still need food. So aim for **tiny wins**:

- "Today I will get out of bed and check the mail."
- "Today I will praise God, regardless of how I feel."
- "Today I will go to the store for a few essentials."
  Small steps are still steps. Every finish line you cross strengthens your soul.

5) Don't Live in Regret

"Hindsight is 20/20." Regret can either chain you to *what was* or teach you how to live *what's next*. Use regret as a **teacher**, not a jailer. (We'll explore this more in the next chapter.)

When Grief Turns Toward Sin

Grief runs long in some seasons, and God is patient. But watch for signs that sorrow has hardened into rebellion or idolatry: an ongoing refusal of God's comfort; contempt for His goodness; chronic self-medication; making the departed the center of life. When you recognize these, **turn**—ask for help from the Lord, your pastor, and wise believers who will walk with you.

Matthew 11:28 – "Come to Me... and I will give you rest."

A Word About Medication and Help

Medicines can sometimes **help stabilize** a person so they can process grief with God and wise counselors; they can also be **overused** in ways that delay necessary processing. The key is **wisdom and humility**: pray, seek counsel, and—if needed—consult a trusted, competent **Christian physician or counselor**. Medication is never our *savior*; Jesus is. But common grace can be part of how He helps us heal. Whatever you choose, do so **prayerfully**, not as a crutch to avoid the heart, and never without wise input.

2 Corinthians 12:9 – "My grace is sufficient for you, for My power is made perfect in weakness."

Walking Forward with Hope

Grief doesn't need to be "overcome" unless it lingers unnaturally long or leads us into sin. In a healthy, spiritually maturing life, grief **eases** as God comforts us. We can help that process by keeping God at the forefront, praising Him in our weakness, and staying **receptive** to His love and mercy.

Remember:

- **God is near.** He binds up broken hearts.
- **You are allowed to weep.** Jesus did (John 11:35).
- **Hope is real.** For believers, death is **gain**, not loss (Philippians 1:21).
- **Heaven is home.** Reunion is ahead (1 Thessalonians 4:13–18).

A Simple Prayer for the Valley

Lord Jesus, You are the Man of Sorrows and acquainted with grief. Hold me when I cannot hold myself. Teach me to receive Your comfort, to tell You the truth about my pain, and to walk one small step at a time. Keep me from idols that numb but cannot heal. Heal my heart, and help me honor You with how I grieve. **Amen.**

A Short Practice for This Week

- **One Psalm a day** (try Psalms 23, 27, 34, 42, 46).
- **One small task** each day (name it, do it, thank God for strength).
- **One person** to text or call for prayer.
- **One memory** to thank God for today.

The God who met Job in his ashes, who wept at Lazarus's tomb, and who rose victorious from His own grave, will **meet you**, too. He will not waste your tears. And one day, He will wipe **every** one of them away.

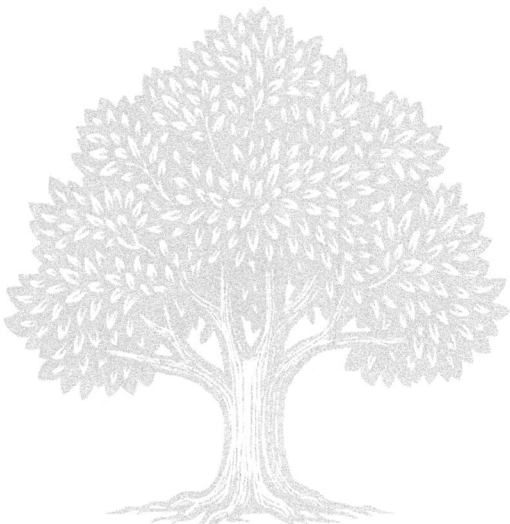

CHAPTER 11
HOW TO OVERCOME
REGRET

Regret has a staggering power. It can either propel you into a wiser future—avoiding the mistakes of the past—or it can keep you bound in a prison of "what if," limiting relationships and stunting spiritual growth. **Which outcome is up to you.**

Regret is unlike most emotions. It is the one feeling we cannot pawn off on someone else. We can say:

- "I'm angry because you forgot my birthday."
- "I'm sad because you hurt me."

- "I'm worried he won't call back."

But regret? By its nature, it points inward. We feel regret because **we** failed to act, chose poorly, or didn't foresee the consequences—and we know it.

Regret ranges in severity:

- *Mild:* "I knew I should've set the alarm earlier—now I'm late."
- *Severe:* "Why didn't I tell my father how I really felt? I wasted the time I had. Now he's gone."

The more severe forms are the ones that paralyze. A classic example is relationships. Many of us have watched a relationship end badly, recovered in time, and moved on. But some carry the pain forward and ask, "Is any new relationship worth risking this kind of pain again?" Often the quiet answer is **no**—so we disengage or refuse to invest emotionally. Regret becomes a wall.

We don't need a psychology lecture to know how regret feels. We need a **path** to redeem it. Here it is.

A Three-Step Path: Admit • Mourn • Leave

1) Admit that regret is holding you back

The first step is honest confession: *"My regret is harming me."* We tell ourselves we're avoiding pain, but too often we're avoiding **love**, **trust**, and **obedience** to God's call.

Common inner vows sound like:

- "She hurt me so badly; I'll never trust like that again."
- "He cheated on me; my next boyfriend won't leave my sight."
- "I got burned helping people; no good deed goes unpunished. Never again."

These vows feel protective, but they are **bars on a cell**. Name them. Renounce them before God. Replace them with truth: *"Lord, You are my refuge. Teach me to love wisely again."*

1 John 1:9 — "If we confess our sins, He is faithful and just to forgive us our sins and to cleanse us from all unrighteousness."
Psalm 32:5 — "I acknowledged my sin to You... and You forgave."

2) Mourn what happened—properly and with God

Many get stuck in regret because they never **grieved** the loss beneath it. They learned to cope, not to heal. God invites you to revisit—not to relive—the wound with Him:

- Identify the loss (the person, the opportunity, the trust).
- Acknowledge you cannot change the past.
- Lament honestly (read Psalms 32, 38, 51; 42–43).

- Ask God to use the experience for good and growth.

Replace the vow *"Never again"* with *"Next time, by God's grace, I will do better."* Godly sorrow is not a cul-de-sac; it **leads somewhere**.

2 Corinthians 7:10 — "Godly grief produces a repentance that leads to salvation without regret, whereas worldly grief produces death."

3) Leave it in the past—on purpose and by practice

There comes a Spirit-led moment to **set it down**. You have dealt with it; you've met God in it; now choose to **leave it**. When old triggers flare:

- Say: *"I've brought this to God. I'm forgiven. I'm learning. This memory cannot rule me."*
- Shift to action: take a small, faithful step the *new* you would take.

This is a favorite place of attack for the adversary. Don't let him reopen what Christ has closed.

Philippians 3:13–14 — "…forgetting what lies behind and **straining forward** to what lies ahead… I press on toward the goal…"
Romans 8:28 — "We know that for those who love God all things work together for good…"

Turning Regret into Wisdom (Practical Tools)

A. The 4R Exercise (10 minutes, pen + paper)

1. **Recognize** — Write the regret in one sentence.
2. **Repent** — What, specifically, do you need to own before God or others?
3. **Repair** — Is there an amends to make? A call to place? A restitution to offer? (Do what is *safe and wise.*)
4. **Re-plan** — Note one concrete practice that would have prevented it. Put that practice on your calendar this week.

B. Truth Swap (for looping thoughts)

- Lie: *"I ruined everything."*
- Truth: *"I sinned/erred, but Jesus redeems. I can walk in newness today."* (Romans 8:1; Lamentations 3:22–23)

C. Accountability
Invite a mature believer to ask you, weekly: *"What regret tried to speak? What truth did you answer with? What obedient step did you take?"*

D. Redeem the Skill
If your regret came from an actual **skill gap** (budgeting, conflict resolution, boundaries), address it: take a course, read a book, meet a mentor. Repentance grows **competence**.

What About Irreversible Regrets?

Some losses cannot be repaired on earth: words unsaid, a life now gone, years wasted. God still meets you **here**.

- **Receive mercy.** Christ's cross is enough even for this.
- **Honor their memory** by how you live now—write the letter you wish you'd written, but to someone still here.
- **Seed the future**—serve where your regret points (mentor a younger believer, reconcile where possible, volunteer where you once stood idle).

Joel 2:25 — "I will **restore** to you the years that the locust has eaten…"

Regret vs. Condemnation

- **Conviction** is specific, hopeful, and invites action.
- **Condemnation** is vague, crushing, and immobilizing.

If your thoughts accuse without a path forward, that's not the Shepherd's voice.

Romans 8:1 — "There is therefore now **no condemnation** for those who are in Christ Jesus."

A Simple Prayer

Father, I bring You my regret. I confess what I did and what I failed to do. Thank You that Jesus' blood is enough for this, too. Teach me to grieve with You, to make amends where I can, and to walk wisely where I once stumbled. I lay down vows that have chained me, and I receive Your mercy and newness. Lead me by Your Spirit to the next faithful step. **Amen.**

This Week's "Next Steps"

- **One amends** (if appropriate): a call, a note, or restitution.
- **One boundary or habit** that would have prevented the regret (implement it).
- **One Scripture** to memorize (choose from above).
- **One person** to tell what you're doing—invite prayer and accountability.

Bottom line: Regret is a **teacher**, not a warden. With Jesus, you can **admit** it, **mourn** it, and **leave** it—walking forward wiser, softer, and freer.

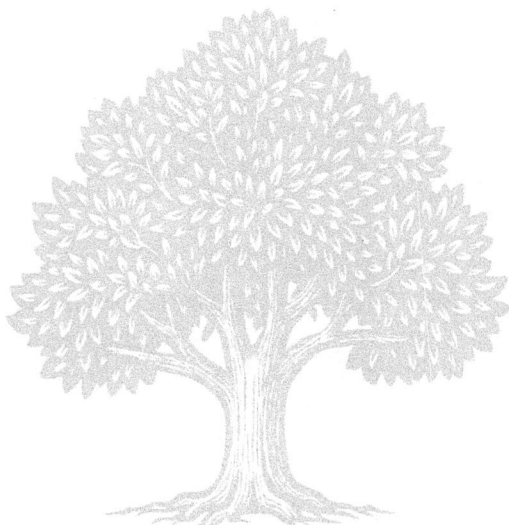

CHAPTER 12
HOW TO PLEASE GOD

As we mature in our walk with God, the question eventually rises: **"Am I pleasing God?"** Another way to ask it is, **"How do I please God?"** The answer is simple, though not always intuitive. In our flesh, we assume we please God by going to church, dropping tithes and offerings in the plate, praying and worshiping, and generally being a "good" Christian.

If that's your assumption, you're not alone. This idea is widespread—and ancient. The author of **Hebrews** addressed the first-century church on this very issue (most scholars date Hebrews to around A.D. 65). So grab your Bible and turn to **Hebrews 11**, because that's where we find the answer.

If you paused and read the chapter, you likely felt it— **God's Word answering the question directly**. If you missed it, here it is:

Hebrews 11:6 (NIV)
"And **without faith it is impossible to please God**, because anyone who comes to Him must believe that He exists and that He rewards those who earnestly seek Him."

The first thing we must have, if we hope to please God, is **faith**. Otherwise, it is **impossible**. No matter how hard we try, nothing we do will please God **without faith**. Faith is the key that unlocks the door.

A Tale of Two Lives

David and **James** are best friends. They were raised similarly by like-minded parents. They attended the same schools, the same church, and grew up to be productive members of society. Both married, had children, held good jobs, gave generously to neighbors and church, raised their families in the faith, and—after long, fruitful lives—both died peacefully in their sleep.

Which man pleased God? On the outside, they look identical, so we might say, *both*. But in this example, only **one** was pleasing to God.

God saw what others couldn't: **David** never developed a personal relationship with Him. He lived by routine. He gave time because that's what "good people" do. He went to church because it was tradition. He raised his family in the same church because that's all he knew.

James, on the other hand, **knew** and **loved** God. He served and gave not because of upbringing alone but because he had **faith**—that God is who He says He is and will do what He says He will do. James brought his children to church because **God** says, *"Train up a child in the way he should go; even when he is old he will not depart from it."* He lived outwardly similar to David, but **the difference was faith and love**. God looks at the **intent**—the heart posture behind the action.

So when we copy the outward behavior of faithful people but do not share their **faith**, it's no surprise we grow frustrated: *"I go to church. I give my money and time. I pray. What more do You want, God?"* Perhaps it's not what you **are** doing, but **why** you're doing it.

Are you doing these things to **earn favor**, or because you **love** God and **trust** Him? The difference may seem subtle to us; it is **massive** to God. If you're doing the right things for the wrong reasons, how do you change that? **Build your faith.**

(That's the focus of the next chapter.) For now, remember: **God loves you, and you're on the right track.** Keep going.

Scriptures to Strengthen Your Faith

Acts 16:31 – "Believe in the Lord Jesus, and you will be saved, you and your household."

Romans 11:20 – "They were broken off because of their unbelief, but you stand fast through faith. So do not become proud, but fear."

2 Corinthians 5:7 – "For we walk by faith, not by sight."

Galatians 2:20 – "I have been crucified with Christ. It is no longer I who live, but Christ who lives in me... I live by faith in the Son of God, who loved me and gave Himself for me."

1 Peter 5:8–9 – "Be sober-minded; be watchful. Your adversary the devil prowls around like a roaring lion... Resist him, firm in your faith..."

1 John 5:4 – "For everyone who has been born of God overcomes the world. And this is the victory...—our **faith**."

A Simple Prayer

Father, I want to please You. Grow in me a living faith—trust that You are who You say You are and will do what You promise. Purify my motives so my obedience flows from love. Teach me to seek You earnestly and to rest in Your reward—**Yourself**. In Jesus' name, **Amen**.

CHAPTER 13
HOW TO FIND FAITH

"Now faith is **confidence** in what we hope for and **assurance** about what we do **not** see." **Hebrews 11:1**

You couldn't ask for a better definition—straight from Scripture. Faith is confident trust and quiet assurance about realities we cannot see. So ask yourself: **What are you hoping for? Do you have assurance in the outcome?**

1 Peter 1:8–9
"Though you have not seen Him, you love Him; and

even though you do not see Him now, you believe in Him and are filled with an inexpressible and glorious joy, for you are receiving the end result of your faith, the salvation of your souls."

Peter's words capture my hope perfectly. **I know that I know** my salvation is secure. Whatever situation I face, God will either **see me through it** or **rescue me from it**. His promises are not abstractions to me:

Isaiah 54:17 – "No weapon formed against you shall prosper."
Luke 20:43 – "The Lord will make my enemies a footstool for my feet."
Psalm 23:4 – "Even though I walk through the valley of the shadow of death, I will fear no evil, for **You are with me**; Your rod and Your staff, they comfort me."

I don't just *believe* these are true—I have **experienced** them. God has walked with me through the valley, and His presence has been my comfort.

A Testimony: The Spider Bite and the Savior

A few years ago, I was installing an exterior pole light. (My first career was in electrical work—taught by my dad. At the time, my small company was just my brother and me.) We were trenching near bushes and trees, rolled around in dirt, finished the job, and went home.

A day later, a small tender bump appeared on my lower thigh. I ignored it. Then (in a burst of poor judgment) I played football with kids *on asphalt in dress shoes,* took a hard fall, and cracked some ribs. Two days of nursing pride and pain later, the bump had quadrupled in size, turning sickly yellow and brown. The ER circled it with a marker, gave antibiotics, and sent me home with "come back if it grows."

It grew—fast. The spot turned dark purple with a black center. Back in the ER, a swarm of doctors concluded it was a **Brown Recluse** bite. The venom had caused significant **necrosis**; the tissue was dying. I was admitted. For five days they threw antibiotics and medications at it. Nothing changed. The swelling and darkening continued. Worst case: cutting away dead muscle to the bone—leaving a severe scar. An extreme long shot: losing the leg.

Friends and family prayed. My church prayed—not merely for "improvement," but for **complete restoration**. Kids from my Sunday school class drew me get-well cards (many featuring truly terrifying spiders that made me laugh).

After seven days, the meds finally began to take hold—but the hospital informed me I had to transition to outpatient IV infusions due to cost. They recommended a central line; I declined and did standard IVs in arms/hands. God introduced me to remarkable people in that cancer infusion center.

When the infusions ended, the swelling receded and left behind what looked like a **deflated, dark balloon** of necrotic tissue. Surgery was likely. My appointment was set for the next day.

That night, I felt what I had felt the entire time: **joy**. Nurses asked, "How are you so calm?" Friends thought I was in denial. But for the first time in my life, I had **fully** placed my trust in God. I accepted that, **whatever** happened, He would be with me and would gain glory. If they took my leg, I would **hop for Jesus**. If they removed most of the muscle, I'd still have my knees to kneel on and praise Him. My prayer wasn't "heal me," but **"Father, Your will be done."**

The next morning, the site looked less deflated, more normal in color, and itched intensely. (If you're squeamish, skim this sentence.) The top layer of skin had become a scaly "cap." Against medical advice— and after a quick call to my mother—I gently removed the hardened layer. Underneath was **new, unscarred, fully formed skin**. The "scales" fell away; beneath them was **restoration**.

I have no doubt **God healed me**.

Isaiah 53:5 – "He was wounded for our transgressions... and **by His stripes we are healed**."

My doctor had no explanation: "If anything else happens, come back." Science had no satisfying account for *dead* tissue returning as new. **Whose report will you believe?** I will believe **the report of the Lord**. Days later, I stood before my church and testified that **God did it**—not me, not the doctors (who tried everything for days without progress), not medicine. **God** brought life to what was dead.

How Faith Grows

Faith is God's **gift** (Ephesians 2:8–9). It starts small, then grows—often **forged in the fire** of trials.

- **In Scripture:** God stood with Shadrach, Meshach, and Abednego in the furnace (Daniel 3:16–18). He held Moses' hand at the Red Sea. He shut the lions' mouths for Daniel.
- **In our lives:** He was with me in that hospital room.

Faith grows as we **connect God's promises** to our own stories. Start with daily needs:

"God, You know I need a place to live, food to eat, and clothing."

When He provides, who gets the **glory**? Our pride wants credit for what we could never have guaranteed.

"I worked for it!"
Where did the **job** come from? The **skill**? The **breath** in your lungs? Trace every good back to the **Giver**.

If you struggle to give God glory for the small things, you will struggle to **expect** Him in the big things. So practice:

- **Credit God** for His daily mercies (James 1:17).
- **Testify** to others—tell how He provided, comforted, opened doors.
- **Refuse** to "explain away" answers to prayer.

C. S. Lewis warned of the enemy's logic in *The Screwtape Letters*—the "heads I win, tails you lose" argument: if a prayer is **not** answered, it "proves" prayer doesn't work; if it **is** answered, we credit "natural causes," so prayer "still doesn't work." Don't buy that lie.

Practical Ways to Seek and Strengthen Faith

1) Hear the Word

Romans 10:17 – "So faith comes from **hearing**, and hearing through the word of Christ."
Read Scripture aloud. Listen to it. Saturate your mind with God's voice.

2) Remember and Record
Keep a **faith journal**. Date, request, outcome. Rehearse God's past faithfulness when new trials come.

3) Testify
Share your stories—big and small. Your testimony feeds your faith and ignites faith in others (Revelation 12:11).

4) Practice Dependence

Pray **first**; plan **second**. Give thanks before the outcome. Choose generosity when it pinches. Obedience grows trust.

5) Join the Cloud of Witnesses

Read Hebrews 11 often. Let their stories tutor your imagination: faith obeys when it cannot yet see.

A Guardrail Against Pride

When God answers, **don't steal the glory**. Pride says, "My effort did this." Faith says, **"The Lord provided; I labored with what He gave."** Give God glory in the small, and watch faith grow for the large—until, under overwhelming odds, the **peace that surpasses understanding** guards your heart and mind (Philippians 4:7).

A Closing Prayer

Father, thank You for the gift of faith. Train my heart to hear Your Word, to remember Your works, to tell Your story. Keep me from pride and from explaining away Your kindness. Grow in me a faith that obeys when I cannot yet see, and make my life a testimony to Jesus, in whose name I pray. **Amen.**

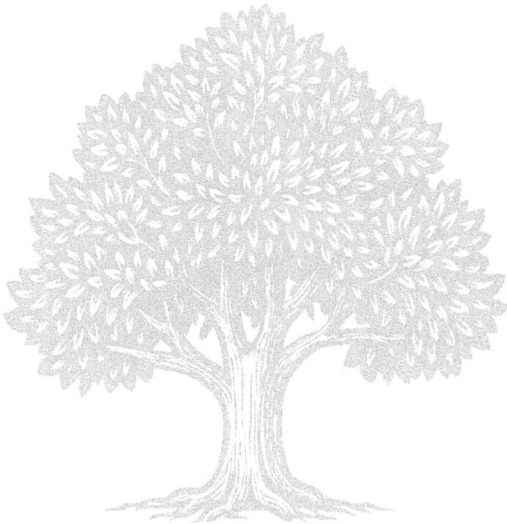

CHAPTER 14
HOW TO BE A GODLY HUSBAND

Wives, if you are reading this and plan on earmarking it for your husband, don't. What you should do is stop reading this chapter and go to the next one, HOW TO BE A GODLY WIFE. It's important to remove the log from your own eye before you point out the splinter in someone else's. Matthew 7:5

Ephesians 5:25
"Husbands, love your wives, as Christ loved the church and gave himself up for her."

Colossians 3:19

"Husbands, love your wives, and do not be harsh
with them."

Ephesians 5:28

"In the same way husbands should love their wives as
their own bodies. He who loves his wife loves
himself."

Ephesians 5:33

"Let each one of you love his wife as himself…"

The Assignment in One Word: Love

Husbands, what are we called to do for our wives?
Love them—**as Christ loved the church.** That is
not the default, feelings-first kind of love our culture
peddles. Christ's love is **supernatural, self-
sacrificing, servant-hearted, and enduring.** That
kind of love is a **choice**—made daily, then practiced
repeatedly.

The world's pattern says: *love her as long as she meets your
needs, remains attractive, doesn't demand too much, doesn't cost
you too much, and doesn't bore you.* Christ calls us higher.

Below are eight qualities of Christ's love. Read the
Scriptures. Pray them in. Practice them at home.

Qualities of Christ's Love (and How Husbands Imitate It)

1. **Unconditional**
   Romans 5:8. Christ loved us while we were still sinners. Under **no** condition does He stop. Your wife must feel secure in your love—especially when she disappoints you. If Jesus' love for you depended on your flawless performance, you would be undone. Love her with that same settled commitment.

2. **Sacrificial**
   1 Peter 3:18; 2:24; Romans 5:6–11; Galatians 2:20; Ephesians 5:2, 25. No one has given more than Jesus. So lay down *self* for your wife—dreams, time, convenience, preferences. Take the job that stabilizes the home. After a long day, jump in: manage the kids for 30 minutes, give her a breather, shoulder chores. When the choice is **me or her**, choose **her**—*every time.* ("...showing honor to the woman as the weaker vessel," 1 Peter 3:7—equal in value, distinct in role.)

3. **Voluntary**
   Ephesians 1:4; John 10:18; 1 John 4:10. No one forced Jesus to love us. Likewise, **choose** to love your wife. Don't be the man who "does the right thing" externally but never chooses love internally. Love is a decision you renew **daily**.

4. **Enduring**
   Romans 8:38; Jeremiah 31:3. Jesus' love is forever. So should yours be. In glory, marriage as we know it ceases, but love does not. Let

your wife hear that your love is not on a timer.

5. **Purposeful**
   Ephesians 5:26. Christ's love sanctifies and builds up. Your love should actively pursue your wife's growth, joy, and well-being—spiritually, emotionally, physically. Everything you do in love should help her flourish.

6. **Intense (but not invasive)**
   John 13:1; Ephesians 5:2, 25–33. Your love should be felt like the steady warmth of a fire—especially in storms. Be **consistent**. Anticipate needs; don't wait to be asked. Serve **cheerfully**, not grudgingly. Intense doesn't mean controlling—give healthy space; reject clinginess or suspicion.

7. **Serving**
   Philippians 2:6–7. Jesus served us. Real husbands are **servant-leaders** at home. Create conditions for your wife to thrive: resources, time, protection, encouragement. Take out the trash, finish the list, put the socks in the hamper—gladly. Help her pursue **her** God-given goals, not only yours.

8. **Obvious**
   John 10:1–14; 14:1–3; 13:34–35; 15:9–10; Romans 8:32; Philippians 4:13,19; Hebrews 4:14–16. Christ's love is unmistakable. Yours should be too—through gratitude, gentle affection, and thoughtful initiative:

• Say *thank you*—specifically and often.

- Leave notes. Hold hands. Open doors. Kiss good morning and good night.
- Pray **with** her and **for** her.
- Send a midday "thinking of you."
- Remember important dates. (Use your calendar. No excuses.)
  When you forget what matters to her, she feels she doesn't matter to you.

Before You Can Be a Godly Husband, Be a Biblical Man

This section is shaped by teaching from Pastor James MacDonald (with adaptations). The command:

1 Corinthians 16:13–14 (ESV)
"Be watchful, stand firm in the faith, **act like men**, be strong. **Let all that you do be done in love.**"

Three "Don'ts"

1. **Don't act like a woman.**
   Men and women are equal in worth, different in design. **Lead**—church, home, family (Romans 12:2). Servant-leadership means carrying responsibility and weight. Don't excuse passivity by blaming a "pushy spouse." Lead humbly.
2. **Don't act like an animal.**
   Beasts run on impulse and territory. You are called to **self-control** and **honor**—at home and everywhere. No crude habits, no "mine!" tantrums. Be a gentleman.
3. **Don't act like a boy.**

1 Corinthians 13:11. Grow up.

- Little boys prioritize games and entertainment over God and marriage. Men don't.
- Little boys talk dirty; men guard their mouths (Matthew 15:18).
- Little boys avoid responsibility; men work and provide (2 Thessalonians 3:10).
- Little boys stay immature; men pursue spiritual, emotional, and practical maturity through Scripture, prayer, mentoring, and goals.

Four Things Real Men Do

1. **Be watchful.**
   1 Peter 5:8. Guard the gates of your home: content, friendships, attitudes. Correct early; don't grant the enemy a foothold.
2. **Be men of faith.**
   Live your convictions. Don't just talk—**do**. Let belief direct behavior. If you are riddled with indecision, your family will be riddled with anxiety.
3. **Be strong.**
   Psalm 31:24. Own your assignment. Admit weakness; receive God's strength. Growth won't be instant, but it will be real.
4. **Do everything in love.**
   You are not a dictator; you're a servant. Correct gently. Discipline without rage (**James 1:20**). Keep love in front of every duty.

This Won't Be Easy—but It Will Be Worth It

Hyper-masculine posturing isn't manhood. Beards, trucks, beer, and bravado don't make men. **Conviction, responsibility, humility, and obedience** do. Train your children now (**Proverbs 22:6**), and by God's grace you'll see generations follow Christ—because you chose to be a man who follows Christ.

You will stumble. Don't lie there and groan. Crawl to the cross, repent, receive correction, and keep going. Don't blame your wife or culture. If she has stepped into leadership, it may be because she couldn't trust your leadership. Rebuild that trust with **consistency** over **time**. A month of effort won't undo years of passivity. Stay steady for as long as it takes.

A Husband's Checklist (with Scripture)

- **Listen with full attention** (Proverbs 25:11).
- **Provide** for her needs—physical, emotional, social, intellectual, sexual, spiritual (1 Timothy 5:8; Ephesians 5:28).
- **Protect** her—set limits, give breathers from demands (Ephesians 5:29; 1 Peter 3:7).
- **Help** her (Ephesians 5:25).
- **Encourage** her (Ephesians 4:29).
- **Sacrifice** for her; choose her will over yours (Ephesians 5:25).
- **Share** life deeply, and invite her to share (1 Peter 3:7).
- **Be satisfied** with her (Proverbs 5:19).

- **Make her first place** under Christ (1 Peter 3:7).
- **Express commitment** (Matthew 19:6).
- **Be tender, courteous, respectful** (Ephesians 4:32).
- **Overlook faults** (1 Peter 4:8; Colossians 3:13).
- **Cherish and appreciate** her openly (Ephesians 5:29; cf. 2 Timothy 3:2—avoid ingratitude).

Key Headship Texts to Ponder

- **Genesis 3:16**
- **Ephesians 5:23–29, 33**
- **1 Corinthians 11:3**
- **1 Timothy 3:4–5**
- **1 Timothy 2:11–14**

A Simple Rule of Life (to actually do this)

Daily (15 minutes):

1. Read a short Scripture with your wife; pray aloud together.
2. Do one tangible act of service she didn't ask for.
3. Speak one specific encouragement about her character or effort.

Weekly:

- 1 unrushed date (phones away).
- 1 family devotion you lead.
- 1 practical support step toward **her** personal goal.

Monthly:

- Review budget and calendar **with** her—plan rhythms that protect marriage, Sabbath, and family.
- Check in on her soul: "How are you *really*? Where can I help?"

Closing Prayer

Father, thank You for loving the church through Your Son. Teach me to love my wife like Jesus—unconditionally, sacrificially, purposefully, and obviously. Make me watchful, steadfast in faith, strong in Your strength, and gentle in all I do. Build our home on Your Word and fill it with Your Spirit. In Jesus' name, **amen.**

CHAPTER 15
HOW TO BE A GODLY WIFE

I want to start this chapter with a warning similar to last chapter. **A word to husbands:** if you're here to thump your wife with this chapter, stop. If your wife is struggling to flourish, first examine your own leadership and expectations. Are they biblical—or selfish? Re-read **How to Be a Godly Husband** before reading further.

Proverbs 31:10
"Who can find a virtuous woman? For her price is far above rubies."

Proverbs 21:19
"It is better to live in a desert land than with a quarrelsome and fretful woman."

A godly wife is first a **godly woman**. By the Spirit, her life bears visible fruit—"love, joy, peace, patience, kindness, goodness, faithfulness, gentleness, self-control" (Galatians 5:22–23). She pursues Christlikeness before she pursues role-perfection.

Also, never underestimate your influence. A husband's confidence is tied closely to his wife's regard. Constant criticism erodes him; wise affirmation strengthens him (Proverbs 14:1).

The Proverbs 31 Pattern (31:10–31)

The Woman Who Fears the Lord
An excellent wife who can find? She is far more precious than jewels.
The heart of her husband trusts in her...
She does him good, and not harm...
She seeks wool and flax...works with willing hands...
She rises while it is yet night...
She considers a field and buys it...plants a vineyard...
She opens her hand to the poor...
Strength and dignity are her clothing...
She opens her mouth with wisdom...
Her children rise up and call her blessed; her husband also, and he praises her...
"Charm is deceitful, and beauty is vain, but a woman who fears the LORD is to be praised."

Core Traits Drawn from Proverbs 31

1. **Trustworthy & honoring.**
   Her husband's heart safely trusts her—
   finances, fidelity, reputation. She "does him
   good," refuses to publicly pick him apart, and
   speaks well of him (vv. 11–12, 23).
2. **Diligent & generous.**
   She works hard—at home and beyond—and
   remains open-handed to the poor (vv. 13–20,
   27).
3. **Balanced beauty.**
   She cares for her appearance without vanity;
   her greater adornment is character (vv. 21–22,
   30).
4. **Capable & enterprising.**
   She can evaluate, plan, purchase, and produce;
   she stewards profit for the household's good
   (vv. 16, 18, 24).
5. **Strong, wise, and joyful.**
   "Strength and dignity are her clothing...she
   laughs at the time to come." Wisdom and
   kindness frame her words (vv. 25–26).

On Biblical Submission

Many objections to submission come from (1) an
ungodly husband, (2) a worldly definition of
submission, or (3) a general resistance to Christ's
authority. Scripture speaks to all three.

1 Peter 3:1–5
"Likewise, wives, be subject to your own husbands,
so that even if some do not obey the word, they may
be won without a word by the conduct of their

wives…with the imperishable beauty of a gentle and quiet spirit…"

1 Corinthians 7:14
"For the unbelieving husband is made holy because of his wife…"

Ephesians 5:21–24
"Submitting to one another out of reverence for Christ…Wives, submit to your own husbands, as to the Lord…"

What Submission Is Not

- It is **not** an admission of inferiority. Men and women are equal in value, distinct in role (Genesis 1:27; 1 Corinthians 11:3).
- It **never** requires sin or lawbreaking (Acts 5:29).
- It is **not** silence in the face of evil. If there is abuse, coercive control, or criminality, seek safety, pastoral care, and lawful help immediately. Submission is not suffering harm in secret.

What Submission Is

- A **Spirit-empowered posture** that honors God's design, freely offered to a husband's loving, Christlike leadership (Ephesians 5:25–33).
- A **continual attitude** (hupotassō—ongoing) that cooperates rather than competes,

contributes rather than controls (Ephesians 5:21–24).

- A **mission alignment**—bringing your gifts, insights, and energy to help the household follow Christ together.

Matthew Henry: "She was not made out of his head to rule over him, nor out of his feet to be trampled upon by him; but out of his side to be equal with him, under his arm to be protected, and near his heart to be loved."

If your husband is not yet godly, submission remains a **witness**, not a surrender of conscience. Pray, set wise boundaries, involve healthy leaders, and keep your hope in Christ. As Ruth Bell Graham said, "It's my job to love; it's God's job to change."

Everyday Practices of a Godly Wife

Heart Posture

- Cultivate a **quiet and gentle spirit** (1 Peter 3:4)—not timid, but peaceable and steady.
- Choose gratitude over grumbling (Philippians 2:14–15).
- Guard the tongue: speak life, not contempt (Proverbs 31:26; Ephesians 4:29).

Toward Your Husband

- **Respect him publicly**; correct him privately (Proverbs 31:23).
- **Encourage his calling**—name evidences of grace you see (Hebrews 10:24).
- **Partner in decisions**—offer counsel, then support the final call unless it's sinful.
- **Practice initiative**—help carry family burdens without keeping score (Galatians 6:2).

Home & Work

- Order the household with diligence (Titus 2:5), and—where fitting—engage enterprise that serves the family's mission (Proverbs 31:16, 24).
- Keep a **generous margin** for mercy: time, table, and tenderness for the needy (v. 20).

Soul Care

- Prioritize Scripture and prayer; you cannot pour from an empty cup (Luke 10:39).
- Anchor identity in Christ, not comparison (Proverbs 31:30; Colossians 3:3).

Common Pitfalls to Refuse

- **Contempt & sarcasm.** They corrode intimacy (Proverbs 21:9, 19).
- **Chronic control.** Help shape, don't seize, leadership (Ephesians 5:22–24).

- **Idleness & distraction.** Beware endless scrolling and comparison (Proverbs 31:27).
- **Appearance-centric living.** Beauty fades; fear of the Lord does not (Proverbs 31:30).

A Simple Rule of Life

Daily (15–20 minutes)

1. Sit with the Lord (Word + prayer).
2. Speak one *specific* encouragement to your husband.
3. Do one unasked act of service for the home.

Weekly

- Plan the calendar and budget **together.**
- Share a prayer walk or date (phones away).
- Extend hospitality—simple is fine.

Monthly

- Review goals: family, ministry, rest.
- Give intentionally to mercy and mission.

Scriptures to Ponder for Godly Womanhood

- **Modesty & holiness:** Proverbs 7:10, 18–23; 1 Peter 3:3–4
- **Truthfulness & gentleness:** Proverbs 7:21–23; 9:13
- **Homeward diligence:** Proverbs 31:13; Titus 2:5; 31:27

- **Service & generosity:** Proverbs 31:15, 20
- **Trustworthiness:** Proverbs 31:11–16
- **Financial wisdom:** Proverbs 31:16, 24
- **Reputation:** Proverbs 31:23, 28; 1 Timothy 3:7
- **Wisdom & strength:** Proverbs 31:25–26

Closing Prayer

Father, make me a woman who fears You more than I fear the future. Clothe me with strength and dignity. Put wisdom on my tongue, kindness in my tone, diligence in my hands, and joy in my service. Teach me to respect my husband, support his calling, and steward our home for Your glory. Guard me from pride, contempt, and idleness. Fill our marriage with Your Spirit, for Jesus' sake. **Amen.**

CHAPTER 16
HOW TO BE A GODLY FATHER

The absence of godly fathers has wounded homes, churches, and communities. Prisons are crowded with men whose stories might have been different had a father loved, taught, and led them. Our adversary aims at the family because fathers are its **keystone**— but abdication is still a choice. God charged men to keep watch (Ezekiel 33:7). Too many left the wall.

This is not to shame; it is to **awaken.** You must feel the weight of the calling so you do not drift into apathy while mothers shoulder a burden God never designed them to carry alone. By grace, failure does not have to be final (Joel 2:25).

"What therefore God has joined together, let not man separate." (Mark 10:9)
"Did he not make them one? … And what was the one God seeking? Godly offspring." (Malachi 2:15)

Hope for a turnaround

If you have fallen short, start now. God delights to rebuild ruins (Isaiah 58:12). One father's repentance can ripple for generations. Think Abraham: one man's faith birthed a nation.

Three beginnings every godly father must make

1. **Decide to be a godly father.**
   Set your face like flint. Fatherhood is not autopilot; it is a **calling** that will regularly put your children's good ahead of your comfort— just as Christ did for His church (Ephesians 5:25).
2. **Become a godly man.**
   You cannot lead your children where you refuse to go. Revisit the chapter on biblical manhood. Pursue holiness, humility, and integrity (Micah 6:8).
3. **Be a godly husband.**
   Your children learn marriage by watching yours. Sons will imitate you; daughters will choose by you. Loving their mother is one of

the most strategic ways you love them (Ephesians 5:25–29).

When the home is broken

If you are divorced

Scripture acknowledges limited grounds (sexual immorality, and abandonment by an unbeliever: Matthew 5:32; 19:9; 1 Corinthians 7:15). Even then, reconciliation should be earnestly sought when possible. Pray for restoration. Where reconciliation is not possible, accept the **consequences** without self-pity and redouble your presence and godliness for your children.

If you were never married

Pursue honorable covenant if the door is open. If it is not, then **maximize presence**: consistent, predictable, sacrificial time. Worship with them weekly. Eat meals together often. Call on days you cannot see them. Be the most reliable person in their world.

In both scenarios, obey court orders; pay support on time. That is not only civil duty—it is **Christian faithfulness** (Romans 13:7). Build a workable relationship with their mother focused on the children's flourishing; let consistency, not speeches, rebuild trust.

The core assignment of a father

"These words…shall be on your heart. **You shall teach them diligently to your children**, and shall talk of them when you sit…walk…lie down…rise." (Deuteronomy 6:6–7)
"Train up a child in the way he should go…" (Proverbs 22:6)
"Fathers, do not provoke your children to anger, but **bring them up in the discipline and instruction of the Lord**." (Ephesians 6:4)

Your job description:

- **Instruct** your children in God's Word.
- **Form** their hearts with loving discipline.
- **Provide** for their minds, bodies, and souls.
- **Model** what you teach—consistently.

As Gangel & Gangel summarize, fathers are instruments in the Lord's hand: God's **authority** and **truth** must meet a child's heart through your words, ways, and warmth. And discipline must be like the Father's—love, grace, mercy, and firmness—never harshness or humiliation (Hebrews 12:5–11).

Martin Luther advised keeping an "apple by the rod"—pair correction with encouragement. Let your children leave every discipline moment knowing what was wrong, what is right, that they are loved, and that reconciliation stands.

Five everyday commitments of a godly father

1. **Be present.**
   Show up early, linger long, and return often. Quantity time creates quality time.
2. **Open the Bible.**
   Read, pray, and talk Scripture at the table, in the car, at bedtime. Keep it simple and regular. Short and daily beats long and rare.
3. **Bless with words.**
   Name what you see God doing in them. Affirm identity ("You are my son/daughter, deeply loved"), not just performance.
4. **Shepherd emotions.**
   Teach your kids to name feelings, bring them to God, and act wisely. Calm is contagious; so is anger (James 1:20).
5. **Train for life.**
   Work alongside them. Teach chores, money, service, repentance, forgiveness, church membership, and mission.

A simple father's Rule of Life

Daily (15–30 minutes)

- Read a Psalm/Proverb and pray *with* your children.
- Ask one open question: "Where did you see God today?"
- Offer one specific encouragement.

Weekly

- Family worship (church + one home devotion).
- One-on-one time with each child (even 20–30 minutes).
- Serve someone together.

Monthly

- Review goals (school, friends, screens, chores).
- Plan an adventure (memory > money).

Guardrails and pitfalls

- **Do not provoke.** Avoid sarcasm, comparison, unpredictable anger (Ephesians 6:4; Colossians 3:21).
- **No abdication.** Screens do not raise children; fathers do.
- **No authoritarianism.** You are not the ultimate authority—God is. Lead under His Word.
- **Seek help early.** If there is addiction, violence, or mental-health struggle, pursue pastoral care and professional help. Love protects (1 Corinthians 13:7). Safety first.

When you've blown it

Repent **to God** and **to your children**. Say the words: "I was wrong. Will you forgive me?" Repentance restores credibility faster than pretending perfection.

Then take the next right step. Keep taking it tomorrow.

A father's prayer

Father, thank You for entrusting these souls to my care. Make Your Word alive in my heart and on my lips. Help me lead with humility, love with strength, correct with wisdom, and delight in my children the way You delight in Yours. Restore what is broken, protect what is good, and let generations after me love Christ more because I was their dad. In Jesus' name, **Amen.**

Key Scriptures (for further meditation)

Deuteronomy 6:1–9; Joshua 24:15; Psalm 78:4–7; Proverbs 1:8–9; 3:11–12; 13:24; 20:7; 22:6; Malachi 4:6; Luke 11:11–13; Ephesians 5:25–29; 6:1–4; Colossians 3:20–21; 1 Thessalonians 2:7–12; 2 Timothy 3:14–17; Hebrews 12:5–11.

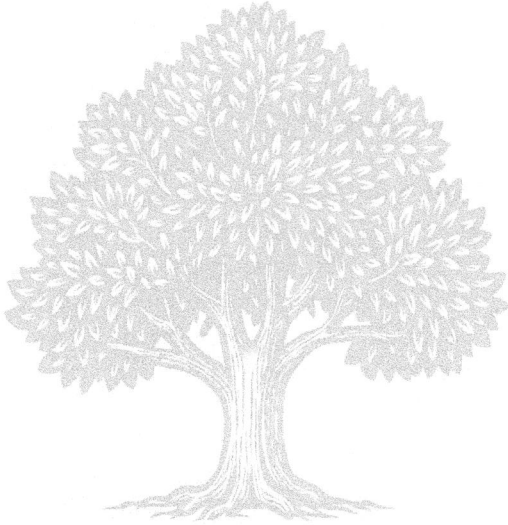

CHAPTER 17
HOW TO BE A GODLY MOTHER

Before we talk about *how* to be a godly mother, we have to start with *who* you are becoming. Mothering flows from identity and discipleship.

1. **Be a godly woman.**
   You can't be a godly mother without first pursuing Christlikeness as a woman. This doesn't happen by accident. It's daily devotion, repentance, obedience, and dependence on the Spirit (Galatians 5:22–23).

Draw near to God; the more you resemble Jesus, the more your mothering will too.

2. **Be a godly wife.**

Likewise, it's impossible to embody biblical motherhood while neglecting your calling as a wife (Ephesians 5:22–24; Titus 2:4–5). Your children are watching. If your words say one thing and your life models another, they will learn conflict, not coherence. Healthy mothering grows best in the soil of a Christ-honoring marriage.

A pastoral word to single mothers

Whether through abandonment, divorce, or death, single motherhood is deeply demanding. Scripture doesn't ignore you; God tells the story again and again of His care for widows and the fatherless (Psalm 68:5; James 1:27). He sees, knows, and supplies.

- **When sin led here:** God forgives freely in Christ (1 John 1:9), yet consequences can linger. His grace is real for you and your children—and for the father—when you all turn to Him (1 Corinthians 7:12–14).
- **When suffering led here:** If you were sinned against or bereaved, the Lord is near to the brokenhearted (Psalm 34:18). He will uphold you.

When possible, foster a peaceful, child-centered relationship with your children's father. If reconciliation and covenant marriage can be pursued safely and biblically, pray boldly toward that end. If not, still encourage regular, appropriate involvement from their father for the children's sake. Put their welfare ahead of your understandable hurts. And pray for him—his salvation, wisdom, work, health, and growth as a father. Those prayers align with God's will.

God's high calling for mothers

Children are a gift (Psalm 127:3–5). In Titus 2:4, Paul uses *philoteknos*—a distinctly maternal love: nurturing, attentive, affectionate, and purposeful. What does that look like day to day?

1) Teach diligently

"You shall teach them diligently to your children ... when you sit ... walk ... lie down ... rise." (Deuteronomy 6:6–7)

Teaching is not occasional; it's a lifestyle. It requires **presence** and **conversation**—processing life under God's Word at breakfast, in the car, after tears, before bed. You and your husband share this sacred task (Psalm 78:5–6; Deuteronomy 4:10).

2) Train intentionally

"Train up a child in the way he should go…"
(Proverbs 22:6)

Training moves beyond information to **formation**—
habits of prayer, Scripture, worship, repentance,
service, and discernment. Help each child discover
their gifts and walk personally with Jesus.

3) Discipline in love

Hebrews 12:5–11 and Proverbs 13:24; 19:18; 22:15;
23:13–14; 29:15–17 all join hands: loving parents
correct consistently for the child's good. Discipline is
never rage, shaming, or chaos. It is **calm, clear,
consistent, and restorative**—paired with instruction
and affection. If you're heated, pause. Correct after
you pray.

4) Nurture the heart

Apply Titus 2:4; 2 Timothy 1:7; Ephesians 4:29–32;
5:1–2; Galatians 5:22; 1 Peter 3:8–9 to your home:
create a climate of **encouragement, acceptance,
affection, and grace**. Give freedom to fail. Be quick
to forgive. Speak life.

5) Model integrity

"Only take care, and keep your soul diligently …
make them known to your children." (Deuteronomy
4:9)

"Whoever walks in integrity walks securely."
(Proverbs 10:9; 11:3)

Children imitate what we *are* more than what we *say*. Let your private life match your public words. When you sin, confess to God—and, age-appropriately, to your children. Repentance in a parent builds deep trust.

Working together with your husband

God appointed fathers as heads of the home, accountable for the family's spiritual, physical, and mental well-being (Ephesians 5:23; 6:4). A godly mother is a **strong helper** (Genesis 2:18)—not a bystander. Align with him, pray with him, and present a united front. If you are carrying this alone, the Lord remains your covering; ask Him for a Titus 2 community to share the load.

Everyday rhythms for godly mothers

Daily

- 10–15 minutes of Scripture and prayer with your children (short and simple beats long and rare).
- One "heart question": *Where did you see God today?*
- One specific encouragement you've noticed.

Weekly

- Worship together at church.
- A family meal with phones away and Bibles nearby.
- One-on-one time with each child (even 20 minutes).

Monthly

- Review chores, screens, friendships, and spiritual goals.
- Serve someone in need together.

Guardrails & good sense

- **No screaming culture.** Anger does not produce righteousness (James 1:20).
- **No favoritism or comparison.** It bruises hearts (cf. Genesis 37).
- **No abdication to screens.** Technology can assist; it must not replace you.
- **Seek help early.** If there is abuse, addiction, depression, or special needs, pursue pastoral care and qualified professionals. Protecting your children is love (1 Corinthians 13:7).

A mother's prayer

Father, thank You for entrusting these children to me. Fill me with Your Spirit. Teach me to teach them, to train with wisdom, to discipline with love, to nurture with tenderness, and to walk with integrity. Knit our family together in Christ. Make our home a small outpost of Your kingdom, for Jesus' sake. **Amen.**

Key Scriptures (for further meditation)

Deuteronomy 4:9–10, 23; 6:6–9; Psalm 127:3–5; 78:4–7; Proverbs 10:9; 11:3; 22:6; 29:15–17; Matthew 18:1–6; Romans 12:9–21; Ephesians 4:29–32; 5:1–2; 6:1–4; Colossians 3:12–17, 20–21; 1 Timothy 2:9–10; Titus 2:3–5; 1 Peter 3:1–9; James 1:19–27.

Epilogue

If you've journeyed through these pages, you've already noticed: I wasn't kidding—this book doesn't have all the answers. There are no quick fixes or shortcuts for life's hardest questions. If you're looking to me, your pastor, or your small-group leader to solve everything, you'll end up disappointed. We're not capable of carrying that weight. Only God is.

What I *can* do—and what I've aimed to do—is point you toward the One who does have answers. Learning to read Scripture, trust its promises, and *apply* its principles in ordinary days and extraordinary storms: that's the heart of this book and of the ones to come. These chapters are not a finish line; they're a trailhead. They won't hand you conclusions; they'll lead you to the place where conclusions are found— at the feet of Jesus.

The gap between *knowing* and *doing* is where many of us live. James says it bluntly: "Faith without works is dead" (James 2:26). But let's not flip that into a new legalism; "all our righteous deeds are like a polluted garment" apart from grace (Isaiah 64:6). Works don't save; Jesus does. Yet living faith *moves*. It obeys. It repents. It forgives. It keeps showing up. When faith breathes, it walks.

Much of what I've written I learned the hard way— sometimes the hardest way. Please don't repeat my mistakes if you can avoid them. Life in a fallen world will never be easy, but it can be anchored. Obeying

God's Word doesn't make the waves stop; it gives you a rock beneath your feet when they rise.

I've shared pieces of my story so you'd see you're not the only one. Henry David Thoreau observed that "most men lead lives of quiet desperation and go to the grave with the song still in them." That does not have to be your story in Christ. You're not alone. "Be imitators of me, as I am of Christ," Paul wrote (1 Corinthians 11:1). The point is not to copy *me*—God forbid—but to aim your whole life at Jesus and follow Him with others who are doing the same.

A simple way to keep going

- **Open the Word daily.** Even ten focused minutes. Read, reflect, respond in prayer.
- **Obey the next obvious thing.** Don't wait for perfect clarity to do the clear command.
- **Gather with believers weekly.** Worship, submit to the Word, take the Supper, serve.
- **Tell someone what God did.** Testimony fuels faith—in you and in them.
- **Ask for help early.** Pastors, counselors, and mature friends are gifts, not last resorts.

A closing prayer

Father, thank You for every truth You've pressed into my heart.
Give me grace to be a doer of the Word and not a hearer only.
Where I'm weary, strengthen me; where I'm proud, humble me;

where I'm afraid, steady me; where I've sinned,
forgive me.
Fix my eyes on Jesus—the author and finisher of my
faith—
and teach me to walk with You, one faithful step at a
time.
In His name, Amen.

If this book has done anything, I pray it has nudged
you closer to Jesus and into the Scriptures. Keep
going. The same Lord who calls you will carry you.

ABOUT THE AUTHOR

Kevin W. Oliver is a storyteller, missionary, and teacher who finds God's fingerprints in ordinary life. A former electrician and small-business owner turned Bible teacher, Kevin writes for everyday believers who want to move from information to transformation. Together with his wife, Karla, Kevin serves as a mission leader and coach with Adventures in Missions (AIM). Their journeys have taken them from mountain villages in Guatemala to quiet retreats back home in Maryland, where the seeds of The Harmonyville Tales first began to grow.—parable-like stories of Bear and Donkey that blend humor, friendship, and gospel truth for readers of every age. For more information, please visit *BearAndDonkey.org*

Disclaimer and References

Pastoral & Practical Guidance (Not Professional Advice)
This book offers pastoral, devotional, and practical guidance from Scripture. It is **not** a substitute for professional care. Always consult qualified professionals regarding:

- **Medical or mental-health needs:** work with your physician or licensed clinician for diagnosis, treatment, and medication decisions.
- **Legal or financial decisions:** seek licensed legal and financial counsel for your situation.
- **Safety:** if you or someone in your home is in danger (including domestic abuse), contact local authorities or a crisis hotline immediately.

Scripture Translations
Unless otherwise noted, Scripture quotations are from the **English Standard Version (ESV)**. Where another translation is used, it is identified in the text.

Quotations & Sources
Select ideas, facts, or quotations in this work are drawn from the following. Page references below refer to the print layout of this edition.

- Pg. 5 — "Two-Week Reading Plan," *New Student Bible* (1992), NIV.

- Pg. 9 — Books of the Bible overview, Blue Letter Bible (overview/synopses).
- Pg. 17 — "How to Get Saved," K. W. Oliver.
- Pg. 39 — Common stressors & physiological effects, WebMD.
- Pg. 46 — Clinical anxiety/panic effects, WebMD.
- Pg. 48 — Sleep paralysis overview, WebMD.
- Pg. 53 — *The Children's Bible*, Henry A. Sherman & C. F. Kent.
- Pg. 67 — *Giving and Tithing*, Larry Burkett.
- Pg. 70 — *Debt-Proof Living*, Mary Hunt.
- Pg. 121 — Sermon concepts/teaching, James MacDonald.
- Pg. 148 — Commentary insight, Matthew Henry.
- Pg. 162; 173 — *Fathering Like the Father*, Gangel & Gangel.
- Pg. 162; 174 — Selected quotations, Martin Luther.
- Pg. CLXXXVI — Henry David Thoreau.

Notes on Fair Use & Permissions
Short, attributed quotations are used for the purposes of review, commentary, or education. For excerpts beyond brief quotations—especially from works under copyright (e.g., C. S. Lewis, Mary Hunt, Larry Burkett, James MacDonald)—publisher permission may be required. All trademarks and copyrights remain with their respective owners.

Bible References for Chapter 9
How to Handle your Finances

God's Ownership & Provision

- Deut 8:18; Haggai 2:8; James 1:17; Ps 15:5; Eccl 7:12; Phil 4:19; Mt 6:31–33; Lk 12:23–24; Jer 29:11

Generosity, Giving & Tithes

- Prov 3:9–10; Eccl 11:1; Lk 6:38; Lk 12:33–34; Mk 12:41–44; Lk 21:1–4; Mal 3:10; Acts 3:6; Acts 20:33; 2 Cor 9:8

Stewardship, Planning & Faithfulness

- Lk 16:9–12; Lk 19:15, 23; Mt 25:18, 27; Lk 14:28; Prov 21:20; Prov 13:11; Prov 22:26–27; Prov 23:4–5

Contentment & Warnings Against Greed

- Heb 13:5; Lk 12:15; Mt 6:19–21, 24; Lk 16:13; Eccl 5:10; Isa 55:2; Php 2:3–4; 1 Tim 6:10–11; Prov 30:8–9

Work, Provision & Family Responsibility

- 1 Tim 5:8; Prov 13:22; Prov 22:7; Mt 6:28; Lam 5:4; Eccl 10:19 (recognizing context)

Wealth's Limits & Eternal Perspective

- Job 28:15; Isa 52:3; Isa 60:9; Isa 65:11–13;
  Ezek 7:19; Isa 46:6; Zech 11:12; Mt 19:21, 24;
  Lk 16:19–31; Acts 8:20

Justice, Honesty & Integrity with Money

- Prov 10:9; Prov 11:3; Mic 3:11; Isa 43:24; Isa
  13:17; 1 Kgs 8:23; Mt 22:21; Jas 1:23

Lending, Interest & Debt

- Exod 22:25; Lev 25:37; Neh 5:10; Prov 22:7;
  Ps 15:5; Lk 19:23

Offerings, Temple/Church Administration & Accountability

- Exod 30:16; Lev 5:15; 2 Kgs 12:4, 7–16; 2 Kgs
  22:7, 9; 2 Chr 24:5, 11, 14; 2 Chr 24:16; 2 Chr
  24:5 (pace/urgency noted)

Narrative/Illustrative Passages Used in Teaching

- **Malachi 3:1–18** (purifying worship; righteous
  offerings)
- **Luke 16:19–31** (rich man & Lazarus; eternal
  stakes of earthly wealth)
- **Mark 12:41–44 / Luke 21:1–4** (the widow's
  offering; heart over amount)

- **Matthew 25:14–30** (talents; faithful stewardship)
- **Luke 12:33–34** (treasure in heaven; heart follows treasure)

Bible References for Chapter 14
How to be a Godly Husband

A husband's primary call: Christlike love & gentleness

- **Eph 5:25–29, 33** — Love as Christ loved; nourish and cherish; love as yourself.
- **Col 3:19** — Love and do not be harsh.
- **1 Pet 4:8** — Love earnestly; love covers a multitude of sins.
- **1 Cor 13:4–7** — Love's character (patience, kindness, endurance).
- **Eph 4:2** — Humility, gentleness, patience, bearing with one another in love.
- **Eph 4:31–32** — Put away wrath; be kind, tenderhearted, forgiving.
- **Prov 25:15** — Patience and a soft tongue persuade.

Headship, servant leadership & spiritual responsibility

- **Eph 5:23–24** — Husband head of wife as Christ of the church.
- **1 Cor 11:3** — Headship order (Christ/man/woman).
- **Col 3:16** — Let the word dwell richly; teach/admonish with worshipful hearts.
- **1 Pet 3:7** — Live in an understanding way; honor your wife; prayers unhindered.

- **1 Tim 4:16** — Watch your life and doctrine closely.
- **Gal 6:2** — Bear one another's burdens; fulfill the law of Christ.

Covenant, unity & priorities in marriage

- **Gen 2:18, 24** — Helper fit; leave, cleave, one flesh.
- **Heb 13:4** — Honor marriage; keep the bed undefiled.
- **Eph 5:1–2** — Imitate God; walk in sacrificial love.
- **Rom 14:19** — Pursue what makes for peace and mutual upbuilding.
- **Eph 4:16** — Joined and held together; each part working in love.

Sexual faithfulness, intimacy & self-control

- **1 Cor 7:2–5** — Mutual conjugal rights; do not deprive; guard against temptation.
- **1 Thess 4:4** — Control your body in holiness and honor.
- **Prov 5:19** — Be intoxicated always in your wife's love.
- **1 Cor 6:19** — Your body is a temple of the Holy Spirit.

Provision, protection & practical care

- **1 Tim 5:8** — Provide for your household.

- **Eph 5:29** — No one hates his own flesh, but nourishes and cherishes it.
- **Phil 2:4** — Look to the interests of others.
- **Eph 6:7** — Serve with goodwill, as to the Lord.

Communication, purity & holiness at home

- **Eph 5:3–4** — Reject impurity, covetousness, filthy talk; embrace thanksgiving.
- **Jas 3:5–6** — The tongue's power and danger.
- **Eph 4:26–27** — Be angry and do not sin; don't give the devil an opportunity.

Forgiveness, reconciliation & peacemaking

- **Eph 4:31–32** — (also above) Kindness, tender hearts, forgiveness in Christ.
- **Matt 5:23–24** *(optional addition in body text)* — Reconcile quickly.

Guarding the home: vigilance & spiritual warfare

- **1 Pet 5:8** — Be sober-minded; watchful against the adversary.
- **Eph 1:21** — Christ's supreme authority (the Leader husbands imitate).

Wise partnering & yoking

- **2 Cor 6:14–15** — Do not be unequally yoked.
- **1 Cor 7:39** — Marry "only in the Lord."

Broader context passages (supportive, not husband-specific)

These can illuminate the chapter's themes (grace, sanctification, mercy, wisdom) and serve group study without being cited as core husband mandates.

- **Prov 31:10–31** — Portrait of an excellent wife (helps husbands honor and encourage).
- **1 Pet 3:1–6** — Wives' conduct (frames mutual honor; paired with 1 Pet 3:7).
- **Gal 2:20** — Life in Christ fuels sacrificial love.
- **2 Cor 12:15** — Spend and be spent in love.
- **Jas 5:16** — Confess and pray; healing in community.
- **Rom 15:1** — Bear with the weak; don't please self.

Bible References for Chapter 15
How to be a Godly Wife

Identity, design & creation order

- **Gen 1:26–27** — Made in God's image, male and female.
- **Gen 2:18, 24** — A helper fit; leave, cleave, one flesh.
- **1 Cor 11:3, 8–9, 7–12** — Headship order; from and for.
- **Gal 3:28** — Equal worth and shared inheritance in Christ.

Core calling: respect, submission, and mutual love

- **Eph 5:22–24, 33; 5:22–33; 5:31–33** — Respect your husband; the church/Christ pattern; one flesh.
- **1 Pet 3:1–6** — Respectful, pure conduct; gentle and quiet spirit.
- **Col 3:18** *(optional to quote in body text)* — Fitting in the Lord.
- **Eph 5:25** *(husband command; frames mutual dynamic)* — His sacrificial love shapes her response.

Character & inner beauty

- **1 Pet 3:4, 6** — Imperishable beauty; fearless trust.
- **Prov 31:10–31 (esp. vv. 10–12, 17, 20–22, 24, 26–28)** — Excellent wife portrait.
- **Prov 12:4; 31:30** — Excellent crown; charm/beauty vs. fearing the Lord.
- **Titus 2:3–5; 2:4** — Older women train younger: love husband/children, self-control, purity, home care, kindness, submission.

Unity, intimacy & faithfulness

- **1 Cor 7:2–5, 3–9, 25–40, 28, 39** — Mutual conjugal rights, self-control, counsel on marriage.
- **Heb 13:4** — Honor marriage; keep the bed undefiled.
- **Prov 5:18–19** — Rejoice in your spouse's love.
- **Eph 5:24** — As the church submits to Christ.

Trust, partnership & household wisdom

- **Prov 31:11–12, 15–16, 20–22, 24, 27–28** — Trustworthy, industrious, enterprising, generous, watchful, praised.
- **1 Tim 5:14** — Manage the household (younger widows instruction).
- **Deut 24:5** — Newlyweds: a year to gladden his wife (priority of home).

- **1 Tim 5:8** *(household provision principle)* — (Husband text) frames shared stewardship.

Honor, prayer & spiritual partnership

- **1 Pet 3:7** — Husbands honor wives so prayers aren't hindered (mutual spiritual care).
- **1 Cor 7:13–16** — Believer's conduct with unbelieving spouse; potential sanctifying influence.
- **Eph 5:31–33** — Mystery and mutuality summarized.

Covenant & permanence

- **Matt 19:9** — Jesus on divorce.
- **Rom 7:2** — Bound while husband lives.

Bible References for Chapter 17
How to be a Godly Mother

Calling & Identity

- **Gen 1:28** — Be fruitful and multiply; steward God's world.
- **Gen 2:18** — A helper fit for him.
- **Prov 18:22** — A wife is a good gift from the Lord.

Creation, Fall & Promise

- **Gen 3:15–19** — Consequences of the fall; promise through the woman's offspring.
- **Gen 3:1–24** — The fall narrative (context).
- **Gen 3:16** — Pain in childbearing; desire and headship.

Character of a Godly Woman/Mother

- **Prov 31:10–31 (esp. vv. 10–12, 23, 27–28)** — Excellent wife/mother: trustworthy, diligent, wise, praised.
- **Prov 14:1** — The wise woman builds her house.
- **Prov 12:4** — An excellent wife is a crown.
- **Prov 16:31** — Gray hair: a crown of glory (righteous life).

Discipleship in the Home (Teach, Train, Model)

- **Deut 6:6–7** *(quoted in the chapter body)* — Teach diligently at all times.
- **Ps 78:5–6** — Teach the next generation.
- **Prov 22:6** — Train up a child in the way he should go.
- **2 Tim 3:16** — Scripture equips for teaching, reproof, correction, training.
- **1 Tim 4:16** — Watch your life and doctrine closely (modeling matters).

Titus 2 Pattern (Mentoring & Domestic Faithfulness)

- **Titus 2:3–5; 2:4–5** — Older women train younger to love husbands/children, be self-controlled, pure, kind, working at home, submissive.

Household Stewardship & Reputation

- **1 Tim 5:10, 14** — Good works, hospitality, caring for the afflicted; younger widows to marry, bear children, manage their households.
- **Prov 31:27** — Looks well to the ways of her household; not idle.
- **Prov 31:23** — Her husband known in the gates (her life strengthens his public standing).

Marriage Context for Motherhood

- **1 Cor 7:1–5, 3–9, 25–40** — Mutuality, conjugal care, counsel on marriage.
- **Eph 5:22–33** — Christ-church pattern informs the home.
- **1 Cor 11:7–9** — Creation order background.

Comfort, Faith & Salvation

- **Rom 8:38–39** — Nothing separates us from God's love.
- **Eph 2:8–9** — Saved by grace through faith.
- **1 Tim 2:5** — One mediator, Christ Jesus.
- **1 Tim 2:15** — "Saved through childbearing" (persevering in faith, love, holiness, self-control).

Gospel Portraits Involving Mothers

- **Luke 1:38** — Mary's faithful submission.
- **Luke 2:10–11** — Good news for all people.
- **John 19:26** — Jesus honors His mother at the cross.
- **Mark 5:34** — "Daughter, your faith has made you well."

Care for Women, Widows & Family Networks

- **1 Tim 5:1–8, 16** — Treat women as mothers/sisters in purity; honor for true widows; family responsibility emphasized.

Broader Context (for extended study)

- **Isa 1:2–20** — God's parental posture toward His wayward children (discipline and invitation).
- **Acts 27:20** — When hope seems lost (useful metaphor for seasons of parenting).
- **John 14:6** — Christ the way, truth, and life (ultimate anchor for family discipleship).
- **Luke 3:38** — Adam "son of God" (biblical family line context).

<u>Notes</u>

<u>Notes</u>

<u>Notes</u>

<u>Notes</u>

Notes

<u>Notes</u>

<u>Notes</u>

<u>Notes</u>

Notes

<u>Notes</u>

<u>Notes</u>

<u>Notes</u>

Notes

www.ingramcontent.com/pod-product-compliance
Lightning Source LLC
Chambersburg PA
CBHW060925040426
42445CB00011B/796